Power Vocabulary Builder
Learning GRE/SAT vocabulary through stories

Volume I

Royal Oxford Language Academy

E. Tan, R.M. Ranken and H. Tan

Table of Contents

Preface

This book series was developed with the objective of helping language learners - especially those who are preparing for the GRE/SAT - master vocabulary words that are commonly found on the test.

Power Vocabulary Builder is the first volume in a language-learning series designed to help you master common GRE/SAT vocabulary. This book is different from those with similar objectives because you'll learn GRE/SAT vocabulary words with the help of 10 mini-stories and extensive practice sets that were developed by English-language experts.

Typically, language learners will learn new vocabulary with the use of a dictionary or flashcards. However, we think that reading stories and learning by association is a much more enjoyable way to learn new words than reading straight out of a dictionary.

Perhaps most importantly, we believe that learning should be fun! We'd like to wish you good luck in your language-learning endeavors, whether or not you are planning to take the GRE or SAT!

Philosophy of this Book

Let's face it, learning a language is hard enough without having to study all of those challenging words for exams like the SAT or GRE. With nearly 200,000 words in the English dictionary, mastering English can seem pretty daunting at times. And on top of that, studying vocabulary can just be downright boring!

That's exactly why we developed this book. We know that none of us *really* have the time or patience to sit down and study a traditional dictionary, so we decided to make learning new vocabulary engaging *and* fun through the use of stories. Getting

a good score on the exam can help set you up for success in your future, and the earlier you start, the better.
This book is the first step toward achieving your goals!

How this Book is Organized

You will be presented with 10 mini-stories that each contain 12 vocabulary words. Each mini-story contains vocabulary that can often be found on standardized tests.

To make it easier for you to learn the vocabulary, we've also developed a section where you'll learn the dictionary definition of each word, synonyms, part-of-speech categories (i.e. noun, verb, adjective or adverb), and several examples of how to use the word in a sentence.

The mastery of any subject requires a great deal of practice. For this reason, we have added a games section in this book. The games will not only help your comprehension, but will also solidify your confidence in the vocabulary!

Most Effective Uses of this Book

To make the most of this book, read the first mini-story and simply try to familiarize yourself with the bolded vocabulary words. These words will most likely new to you, but don't worry -- that's to be expected if English is not your first language!

Once you develop some comfort with the vocabulary words in the story, we suggest that you do the included games and exercises to help further build confidence in your understanding. The first volume of this book comes with a dictionary complete with proper pronunciations, synonyms, antonyms and more, so you can always review words you still aren't comfortable with.

Next, re-read the story until you feel confident in your understanding of each word. (A good marker of this is asking yourself whether you can explain the meaning of the word to another person.) And finally, after you've read a couple of the stories, you can dive into the games and practice sets.

If you are studying for the SAT or GRE, you can best utilize this book by reading two stories per day for approximately one month. Each story contains about 12 vocabulary words, so you'll have learned around 500 new words if you complete the series!

You don't need to worry too much about memorizing the meaning of each word – just focus on understanding the story and the context of each word. You can even try integrating the vocabulary words into your daily conversations for extra practice!

We also highly recommend that you read newspaper articles to expand your vocabulary. This is excellent for practice because it can help you see how applicable these vocabulary words can be in your everyday life. Here are a few great examples:

Vocab: viscous
*"In the case of frog saliva, the faster it is forced to flow, the looser it gets. When the frog tongue hits a cricket, the saliva becomes 100 times less **viscous** and flows around the cricket into every little crevice."*

The New York Times

Vocab: salubrious
*"Delta: 'They are experimenting and have a partnership with LUVO,' a prepared food company that focuses on antibiotic-free proteins and non-GMO and organic ingredients. The airline also unveiled its **salubrious** Flight Fuel program in June. Sample dish: the mesquite-smoked turkey combo."*

The Washington Post

Stories

The Patent Office

By Christina Benson

Young Albert Einstein was a **pedantic (academic)** fellow who often went into **verbose (flowery)** explanations of his thought experiments to anyone who had **inadvertently (rashly)** tried to make small talk with him at his job in the patent office.

At the time, Albert found himself in a frustratingly **disenfranchised (helpless)** position. Although he had graduated from the Zurich Polytechnic Institute, he had not been able to find a teaching job to **culminate (wrap up)** his academic achievements.

Albert spent his days **gleaning (extracting)** new ideas from his **nebulous (vague)** brainstorming sessions. He was **accustomed (used to)** to spending his time **unadulterated (spotless)** by anything but his own thoughts, and waited in a **docile (gentle)** manner for the next stage of his life. He had no idea that one day his contributions to physics would **complement (accompany)** those of Isaac Newton and revolutionize the entire practice, or that he would be held as an **effigy (icon)** to the scientific world for generations to come.

Vocabulary: pedantic • verbose • inadvertently • disenfranchised • culminate • gleaning • nebulous • accustomed • unadulterated • docile • complement • effigy

The Olympia Club

By Christina Benson

In order to get through the monotony of life as a **denizen (inhabitant)** in the patent office, young Albert Einstein established a **cabal (group)**, which he called "The Olympia Club." The club held **sporadic (occasional)** meetings every so often in which they discussed topics including science and philosophy.

Albert, of course, was **seething (teeming)** with ideas. He thought about things like electricity, magnetism, time and space, and the very nature of the universe which he found to be so **exhilarating (exciting)**. He wrote down every single **errant (straying)** thought he had so that he could later share it with his peers in the Olympia Club. He thought of the universe as a **pristine (perfect)** but complex system, whose inner workings could be expressed with elegant, yet simple principles.

Although Albert had become **accustomed (used to)** to his ordinary life at the patent office, his time spent with The Olympia Club was **auspicious (promising)**. He would eventually go on to publish *The Special Theory of Relativity* in 1905. At this point in time, it was as if Albert was held in **lien (legally bound)** of the world as we know it through this grand contribution. Just as he began to question the frameworks of physics, his contributions **forebode (predicted)** their own **invidious (causing animosity)** conclusions from posterity.

Vocabulary: denizen • cabal • sporadic • seething • exhilarating • errant • pristine • accustomed • auspicious • lien • forebode • invidious

The Wonderful Year

By Christina Benson

Albert Einstein was not an **ascetic (austere)** man. He could not find a teaching job because he had not yet completed his higher education by this point, but he felt that he had something even better in store. What he had was a burning curiosity and an imagination that served as a clever **ploy (scheme)** to **burnish (furbish)** his *Special Theory of Relativity* to perfection.

Albert had no intention of **succumbing (giving in)** to the status quo or letting his curiosity lay **dormant (asleep)**, even if it meant **disobeying (disregarding)** the traditional path to success. He found the very idea **mendacious (deceitful)** and **appalling (shocking)**; it was untrue to his nature.

And so he worked day and night, constantly thinking about the concepts of time and space. He considered that perhaps time and space were **porous (sponge-like)**, like a sponge, or that perhaps they were **tangential (unrelated)**, branching off into infinite directions? He stretched the bounds of **sensory (being of the senses)** perception, feeling that the information received by the senses was merely a small piece of the whole picture.

Albert eventually did graduate from the Zurich Polytechnic Institute in 1900, and it was only five years later that he would gather enough mathematical evidence to **substantiate (justify)** the publication of his *Special Theory of Relativity*.

Vocabulary: ascetic • ploy • burnish • succumbing • dormant • disobeying • mendacious • appalling • porous • tangential • sensory • substantiate

Three Brothers: Introduction

By Samantha Andrus

There were once three brothers, each raised by the same two people, yet each very different. The oldest of the three, Steven, was quite **vociferous (loud/forceful)**; he did not care how disruptive he was when it came to expressing his opinions or feelings. When the youngest of the three brothers was born, Steven felt as if though he had been **superseded (replaced)**. He felt that there was no longer a place for him.

Many described John, the middle child, as **staid (unadventurous)**, yet he did not think of himself as boring or old-fashioned by any means. He felt instead that he was an **artful (cunning)** person, and used this characteristic to get his way most of the time. John was also a skilled writer but the speeches he wrote tended to contain so much **bombast (fluff/lack of substance)** that all anyone ever got from them was arrogance.

Many felt that the youngest of the three brothers, Thomas, could be easily **cajoled (persuaded)**. They said that you could talk him into doing just about anything.

When the brothers were together, Steven and John would **censor (delete parts)** their words so that Thomas would not understand. This behavior usually **nettled (annoyed)** Thomas to the point that he would leave the room in a **profound (intense)** manner. Steven would often **admonish (reprimand)** and **objurgate (scold)** Thomas for anything that he did wrong, which left Thomas feeling very spiteful.

As the brothers grew older, Steven and John became increasingly **leery (cautious)** of Thomas rebelling because of the things that they would do to him.

Vocabulary: vociferous • superseded • staid • artful • bombast • cajoled • censor • nettled • profound • admonish • objurgate • leery

Three Brothers: Steven

By Samantha Andrus

Steven was the **precursor (oldest/predecessor)** to his two younger brothers. As he grew older and became **emaciated (skinny)** to the point that he was unable to stand for very long, he often thought of his brothers.

As he **lolled (relaxed)** in his **tawdry (gaudy)** but comfortable chair, he thought about all of the things that he had done to Thomas **wittingly (knowingly)** when they were growing up. He thought about how he would **abase (humiliate)** Thomas at every chance he got, and about how it must have made him feel horrible. He wondered if Thomas was still as **tractable (persuadable)** now as he was when he was young. Steven thought about how he would utilize such **usury (unreasonably high rates on a loan)** against Thomas that, for example, when a loan was paid off, Thomas would have nothing left for himself.

As Steven lay there, reminiscing about the past with a **somber (dark)** expression on his face, he began to feel as though he were simply a lesser man who tried to **emulate (imitate)** greatness when he was younger. This thought **tarnished (ruined)** his mood to the point that not even his **demure (modest)** wife, who sat by his side holding his hand, could make him feel better.

Vocabulary: precursor • emaciated • lolled • tawdry • witting • abase • tractable • usury • somber • emulate • tarnished • demure

Three Brothers: John

By Samantha Andrus

As John grew older he became more **perfidious (deceitful)**, and not many people felt that they could trust him anymore. He became the type of person that had absolutely no problem **thwarting (defeating)** someone in order to make himself look better. He did not often think about anyone but himself or about getting what he wanted. John was once married, but he **curtailed (restricted)** his wife's liberties to the point that eventually she divorced him.

During the divorce, John's **enormous (huge)** eyes were **saturated (wet)** with tears. He tried to get her to stay, but she saw right through his **latent (concealed)** plan. Perhaps his intentions were not as well-hidden as he had thought. When this tactic failed him, John became **ostentatious (pretentious/conspicuous)** and began **vituperating (criticizing)**. This **imperious (overbearing)** behavior made his wife feel as though he were blaming her, so she decided to put up an **impregnable (strong)** barrier between them and decided to **bilk (cheat)** him out of every last penny that he had. To this day, John sits alone in his **gaudy (showy)** home with no one to share it.

Vocabulary: perfidious • thwart • curtailed • enormous • saturated • latent • ostentatious • vituperate • imperious • impregnable • bilk • gaudy

Three Brothers: Thomas

By Samantha Andrus

Thomas, the youngest of the three brothers, was teased mercilessly growing up. Even though he had not seen his brothers in quite some time, he did think about them every once in a while.

When Thomas was growing up he was very easy to deceive. However, now he had grown up to become a very successful lawyer. For every case that he took, he was sure to **substantiate (prove)** the allegations so that the jury would return with a **verdict (judgment)** in his favor.

Thomas married a very **mystique (appealing)** woman whom he found fascinating. The two of them **complemented (supplemented)** each other well; where one fell short the other prevailed.

Thomas did not believe in engaging in **derogatory (disrespectful)** behavior or **coercing (pressuring)** someone into doing anything they did not want to do. He never **blatantly (clearly)** lied about anything and was not an **irascible (quick-tempered)** man. His wife loved him dearly for those reasons.

One night when Thomas came home from work feeling tired and **lethargic (sluggish)**, he spoke with his wife about how he had felt **bereaved (deprived of a loved one)** by the actions of his brothers. However, as the conversation went on they both agreed that it would be quite a **viable (feasible)** idea to organize a reunion, and Thomas began to feel **exhilarated (happy)** by the thought of confronting his brothers again.

Vocabulary: substantiate • mystique • complement • coerce • derogatory • blatant • irascible • lethargic • bereaved • viable • exhilarated

Three Brothers: The Reunion

By Samantha Andrus

After years of separation, the day of the reunion had finally come. All three of the brothers felt **anxious (eager)** about what this day would bring.

Steven was **distraught (worried)**. He felt as though he should find a way to make **reparation (amends)** towards Thomas for all of the horrible things he did to him when they were growing up. John, who **disenfranchised (deprive someone of)** himself after his divorce, felt that he should **emulate imitate)** the younger version of himself. Thomas simply felt **compassionate (loving)** towards his bothers and could not wait to see them.

When the three of them were finally together, they talked about what their lives had brought them: their wives, their children and the like. Thomas told his brothers about his **latent (hidden)** talent for being a lawyer. They looked at some old black-and-white photos that were **juxtaposed (mixed)** with color images, and after a while the discussion brought them back to their childhood.

Steven told Thomas that he was sorry about how he had treated them while they were growing up and how horrible it made him feel. Thomas replied that if it wasn't for Steven pushing him as hard as he did, he certainly would not have become as successful in his career.

At this point, John's **repugnance (disgust)** was growing out of control and one could have sworn that **talons (claws)** were growing right out of his hands. With a deep, **resonant (deep)** growl, John told the two of them just how naïve and **parochial (small-minded)** he thought they were being.

Vocabulary: anxious • distraught • reparation • disenfranchised • emulate • compassionate • latent • juxtaposed • repugnance • talons • resonant • parochial

The First First Lady

By Christina Benson

Eleanor Roosevelt was quite a pivotal figure in history. It was her **zeal (diligence)** as a champion for human rights that changed the nation's view of what a First Lady was. Eleanor refused to accept **chauvinism (sexism)** or the general **malevolent (sinister) flouting (disregard)** of basic human rights. She believed that human rights were **irrefutable (indisputable)**, and devoted her political career to advocating for them.

Orphaned at age 10, Eleanor had no one to **dote (fawn over)** on her from an early age, but she did not let that **impair (damage)** her will to live in any way, and she became strong and independent. She worked hard to **acquaint (present)** herself as an **avid (devoted)** political spokesperson, and to achieve the **tangible (perceivable)** yet **colossal (huge)** goal of equality for all. Her most famous achievement was the Universal Declaration of Human Rights, drafted in 1947.

Her dedication to human rights was part of the **caulking (building blocks)** in the foundation of our great nation.

Vocabulary: zeal • chauvinism • malevolent • flout • irrefutable • dote • impair • acquaint • avid • tangible • colossal • caulk

Sacagawea

By Christina Benson

The journey of Lewis and Clark began after **tractable (compliant)** discussion between Meriwether Lewis and William Clark, and Sacagawea's husband, Toussaint Charbonneau. Sacagawea was a **beguiling (charming)** woman who was seldom **admonished (scolded)** for **effrontery (arrogance)**. She learned early on to be compliant when, as a child, she was taken captive by the Hidatsa tribe. Although she had been **distraught (distressed)** by the experience, overall it helped to **buttress (reinforce)** her sense of self-preservation.

Now as they set off, Sacagawea's mood **oscillated (fluctuated)** from exhaustion by the **laborious (strenuous)** nature of the trip, to exhilaration at the sense of adventure. She gave little thought to the **bourgeois (materialistic/well-to-do)** leaders of the expedition and their **bestial (barbarous)** opinions of her people, or the prospect of **abject (hopeless)** misery that would inevitably fall upon them. She was a woman of indomitable will and spirit — qualities that this journey would only serve to **reiterate (echo)**.

Vocabulary: tractable • beguiling • admonish • effrontery • distraught • buttress • oscillate • laborious • bourgeois • bestial • abject • reiterate

Dictionary

abase [ə'beɪs]

Definition [*verb*]: Cause to feel shame; hurt the pride of
Synonyms: humiliate, mortify, chagrin, humble
Examples:
- "The brother of Louis XVII! How inscrutable are the ways of providence — for what great and mysterious purpose has it pleased heaven to **abase** the man once so elevated, and raise up him who was so abased?"
- "I'm ashamed!" he said, without reserve, **abasing** himself. "I'm utterly ashamed. I'd give anything to be able to undo it."
- "I **abase** myself in apology, Excellency. It was written in the exasperation resulting from ten days in that horrible prison."
- Have I committed an offence in **abasing** myself that ye might be exalted, because I have preached to you the gospel of God freely?
- To **abase** wealth was, according to Madame de Portenduere's ideas, to elevate the nobility and rob the bourgeoisie of their importance.

abject ['æbdʒɛkt]

Definition [*adj*]: Of the most contemptible kind
Synonyms: low, low-down, miserable, scummy, scurvy
Definition [*adj*]: Most unfortunate or miserable
Definition [*adj*]: Showing utter resignation or hopelessness
Synonyms: unhopeful
Definition [*adj*]: Showing humiliation or submissiveness
Examples:
- COURTECUISSE (Madame), wife of the preceding; in **abject** fear of the miser, Gregoire Rigou, mayor of Blangy, Burgundy.
- "A characteristic, but not exactly complimentary, congratulation," returned Laurie, still in an **abject** attitude, but beaming with satisfaction.
- "Off, **abject**!" said Tressilian, striking himself free of Lambourne's grasp; "darest thou come betwixt me and mine enemy?"

- "Don't be **abject**!" cried the Princess. "In a house like this the fastenings are certainly flimsy; they will easily yield."
- "I'm a low, **abject** creature, Vanya," he began. "Save me from myself. I'm not crying because I'm low and abject, but because through me Natasha will be miserable. I am leaving her to misery . . . Vanya, my dear, tell me, decide for me, which of them do I love most, Natasha or Katya?"

accustomed [ə'kəstəmd]

Definition [*verb*]: Make psychologically or physically used (to something)
Synonyms: habituate, accustom
Definition [*adj*]: (often followed by `to') in the habit of or adapted to
Antonyms: unaccustomed
Definition [*adj*]: Commonly used or practiced; usual
Synonyms: customary, habitual, wonted
Examples:
- She was obliged to accustom herself to disrepute, as she had **accustomed** herself to indigence. Gradually she decided on her course. At the expiration of two or three months she shook off her shame, and began to go about as though there were nothing the matter. "It is all the same to me," she said.
- "Yes," she said, "and I am wrong. One ought not to **accustom** oneself to impossible pleasures when there are a thousand demands upon one."
- Then there is no use in trying to **accustom** yourself to their beauty. But we don't find it beautiful. I too have failed to find beauty in them.
- "Because your trial has yet been too short to prove your firmness, and because there is nothing to which time cannot contentedly **accustom** us."

acquaint [ə'kweɪnt]

Definition [*verb*]: Cause to come to know personally
Synonyms: introduce, present

Definition [*verb*]: Make familiar or conversant with
Synonyms: familiarize
Definition [*verb*]: Inform
Examples:

- Bonarmo said, that he must consider of the proposal, and would **acquaint** him with his determination before the following evening.
- I repeated my offers to write to any of her friends; and told her, that, having taken the liberty to **acquaint** Dr. H. with the cruel displeasure of her relations, as what I presumed lay nearest to her heart, he had proposed to write himself, to acquaint her friends how ill she was, if she would not take it amiss.
- He and I parted with great and even solemn tokens of affection; but yet not without gay intermixtures, as I will **acquaint** your Lordship.
- Well, my dearest life, what say you to your uncle's expedient? Shall I write to the Captain, and **acquaint** him, that we have no objection to it?
- The dear creature has thus far condescended — that she will write to Miss Howe and **acquaint** her with the present situation of things.

admonish [æd'mənɪʃ]

Definition [*verb*]: Admonish or counsel in terms of someone's behavior
Synonyms: warn, discourage, monish
Definition [*verb*]: Warn strongly; put on guard
Synonyms: caution, monish
Definition [*verb*]: Take to task
Synonyms: reprove
Examples:

- They said, 'It is the same to us if thou **admonish** or art not of those who 'do admonish; this is nothing but old folks' fictions, for we shall not be tormented!'
- And I myself also am persuaded of you, my brethren, that ye also are full of goodness, filled with all knowledge, able also to **admonish** one another.
- **Admonish** therewith those who fear that they shall be gathered unto their Lord; there is no patron for them but Him, and no intercessor; haply they may fear.

- D'Arnot coughed. The policeman looked up, and, catching his eye, raised his finger to **admonish** silence. D'Arnot turned back to the window, and presently the police officer spoke.
- Let him **admonish**, let him teach, let him forbid what is improper! He will be beloved of the good, by the bad he will be hated.

anxious ['æŋkʃəs]

Definition [*adj*]: Eagerly desirous
Synonyms: dying
Definition [*adj*]: Causing or fraught with or showing anxiety
Synonyms: nervous, queasy, uneasy, unquiet
Examples:
- Anxious for Eager. "I was **anxious** to go." Anxious should not be followed by an infinitive. Anxiety is contemplative; eagerness, alert for action.
- 'Unfortunately I am engaged tomorrow morning,' said Coningsby, 'and yet I am most **anxious**, particularly anxious, to see Millbank.'
- They were **anxious**, terribly anxious, and fierce. Their ferocity wanted something, and they were waiting the moment. And their ferocity was ready to leap out into a mystic exultance, of triumph. But still they were anxious.
- "I don't think that I have been cross; but I am **anxious**, specially anxious. There are reasons why I have to be very anxious in regard to you, and why you have to be yourself more particular than others."
- "And don't again say it's your being **anxious**!" Dennis sprang up warningly. " It's your being anxious that just makes my right."

appall [ə'pɔl]

Definition [*verb*]: Strike with disgust or revulsion
Synonyms: shock, offend, scandalize, appall, outrage
Definition [*verb*]: Fill with apprehension or alarm; cause to be unpleasantly surprised
Synonyms: dismay, alarm, horrify

Examples:

- "Somebody who knows about Mary Clarkson," he considered. "Or Mary herself talking to astonish and **appall**. As she does at times. Or someone who saw a chance of making mischief. . . . And so, what are we going to do?"
- Very funny, your Highness — amazing jolly! And from my nethermost soul, would to Oro, thou could'st but feel one touch of that jolly woe! It would **appall** thee, my Right Worshipful lord Abrazza!
- An intense horror thrilled through the echo of the word; but she rose, and moved, and faced him with the fearless resolve of a woman whom no half-truth would blind, and no shadowy terror **appall**.
- Lightnings, that shew the vast and foamy deep, the rending thunders, as they onward roll, The loud, loud winds, that o'er the billows sweep — Shake the firm nerve, **appall** the bravest soul!
- "This," he exclaimed, with wild gestures, "is enough to **appall** me! Yes, I have bitter enemies, envious rivals who would give their right hand for this execrable letter. Ah! if they obtain it they will demand an investigation, and then farewell to the rewards due to my services.

artful [ˈartfəl]

Definition [*adj*]: Not straightforward or candid; giving a false appearance of frankness
Synonyms: disingenuous
Antonyms: ingenuous
Definition [*adj*]: Marked by skill in achieving a desired end especially with cunning or craft
Antonyms: artless
Examples:

- Yet a few minutes more: he takes her rook and checks again. She literally trembles now lest an **artful** surprise she has in store for him shall be anticipated by the **artful** surprise he evidently has in store for her.
- 'I am afraid,' said Mr. Pecksniff, pausing at the door, and giving his head a melancholy roll, 'I am afraid that this looks **artful**. I am afraid, Mrs. Lupin, do you know, that this looks very **artful**!'

- "I've had some very narrow escapes of being taken in and done for as neatly as you please. There are some **artful** dodgers, whose artful dodging the oldest hand can scarcely guard against; but I'm proud to say not one of those artful dodgers has ever yet been able to get the better of me. Perhaps my time is to come, and I shall be bamboozled in my old age."
- Jeanne followed the priest's **artful** device, and, a fortnight later, told Julien she thought she was enceinte. He started up.
- "The **artful** little woman!" he said, smiling (with reference to Lucetta's adroit and pleasant manoeuvre with Elizabeth-Jane).

ascetic [əˈsɛtɪk]

Definition [*noun*]: Someone who practices self-denial as a spiritual discipline
Synonyms: abstainer
Definition [*adj*]: Pertaining to or characteristic of an ascetic or the practice of rigorous self-discipline
Synonyms: ascetical
Definition [*adj*]: Practicing great self-denial
Synonyms: ascetical, austere, spartan
Examples:
- To mingle with one's life a certain presence of the sepulchre — this is the law of the sage; and it is the law of the **ascetic**. In this respect, the **ascetic** and the sage converge. There is a material growth; we admit it. There is a moral grandeur; we hold to that. Thoughtless and vivacious spirits say…
- Suvarnanabha adds that a woman who passes the life of an **ascetic** and in the condition of a widow may be considered as a sixth kind of Nayika.
- At this moment a man of **ascetic** aspect, with a cold deep eye and not much hair, entered, took hat and umbrella from a chair, and went out.
- But when we compare the military type of self-severity with that of the **ascetic** saint, we find a world-wide difference in all their spiritual concomitants.

- "He is an old man, very learned, and of **ascetic** habits, but he is all indulgence. It will be a sad day when we lose him."

auspicious [ɔ'spɪʃəs]

Definition [*adj*]: Auguring favorable circumstances and good luck
Antonyms: inauspicious
Examples:
- The double entendre is from the proper names Budúr and Su'ád (Beatrice) also meaning "**auspicious** (or blessed) full moons."
- At the present time the Germans say Prosit! under like circumstances. This of course reminds one of the Greek custom of regarding sneezing as an **auspicious** omen.
- I hid my satisfaction. Fate was truly **auspicious**. I would make good use of his absence. There was nobody else in the house whose surveillance I feared.
- The beginning was not **auspicious**, and further progress in conversation seemed to be difficult. "They told me yesterday that Dr. Pullbody was attending you."
- Zhao Zhi thought a moment and replied, "It is an **auspicious** dream. Dragon and Jilin both have horns on the head. It augurs transformation into an ascending creature."

avid ['ævɪd]

Definition [*adj*]: (often followed by `for') ardently or excessively desirous
Synonyms: devouring, esurient, greedy
Definition [*adj*]: Marked by active interest and enthusiasm
Synonyms: zealous
Examples:
- Closer was the wailing; again that faint tremor quivered over the place. And now I caught it — a quick and avid pulsing.
- Once more the pulse, the **avid** throbbing shook the crater. And as swiftly in its wake rushed back the stillness, the silence.

- Constantly in the company of children or smugly respectable women the governess could know little of the world save from an **avid** but limited reading and the sordid gossip of servants.
- Now there was a movement — far, far away; a concentrating of the lambency; the dead-alive swayed, oscillated, separated — forming a long lane against whose outskirts they crowded with **avid**, hungry insistence.

beguile [bɪ'gaɪl]

Definition [*verb*]: Influence by slyness
Synonyms: juggle, hoodwink
Definition [*verb*]: Attract; cause to be enamored
Synonyms: capture, enamour, trance, catch, becharm, enamor, captivate, charm, fascinate, bewitch, entrance, enchant
Examples:
- Then Hallblithe cast himself adown on the grass and said: "I am accursed and **beguiled**; and I wander round and round in a tangle that I may not escape from. I am not far from deeming that this is a land of dreams made for my **beguiling**. Or has the earth become so full of lies, that there is no room amidst them for a true man to stand upon his feet and go his ways?"
- Miss McCroke went on talking and arguing with Rorie, with a view to sustaining that fictitious cheerfulness which might **beguile** Vixen into brief oblivion of her griefs. But Vixen was not so to be **beguiled**. She was with them, but not of them. Her haggard eyes stared at the fire, and her thoughts were with the dear dead father, over whose newly-filled grave the evening shadows were closing.
- Verily, the promise of God is true! Say, 'Let not the life of this world **beguile** you; and let not the beguiler beguile you concerning God.'
- If stumbling is continuing then a side-walk is restoring. If a side-walk is restoring then eating is satisfying. If eating is satisfying then undertaking is **beguiling**. If undertaking is beguiling then shooing is concentrating. If shooing is concentrating then resounding is destroying. That is the way to sleep.

- 'Suit him! They're the scandal of our streets.' Victor was pricked with a jealousy of them for **beguiling** him of his trusty servant.

bereave [bɪ'riv]

Definition [*verb*]: Deprive through death
Examples:
- And God Almighty give you mercy before the man, that he may send away your other brother, and Benjamin. If I be **bereaved** of my children, I am bereaved.
- Thenceforth another than Sueela slept in a hut with a Queen who did not sleep, who, of all the **bereaved** and solitary, was the deepest bereaved and lost in solitude.
- "What is it you fear?" he said impatiently. "To whom, think ye, is your life of such consequence, that they should seek to **bereave** ye of it?"
- So will I send upon you famine and evil beasts, and they shall **bereave** thee: and pestilence and blood shall pass through thee; and I will bring the sword upon thee. I the Lord have spoken it.
- And I will fan them with a fan in the gates of the land; I will **bereave** them of children, I will destroy my people since they return not from their ways.

bestial ['bɛstʃəl]

Definition [*adj*]: Resembling a beast; showing lack of human sensibility
Synonyms: beastly, brute, brutish, brutal
Examples:
- There she sat, unconscious of the glimmer of the firelight, feeding as a beast will bleeding after a blow. Beast she was, with the **bestial** faculty of cherishing a long revenge, with **bestial** treachery and seeming unconcern.
- They might do as they liked — this she realised as she went to sleep. How could anything that gave one satisfaction be excluded? What was degrading? Who cared? Degrading things were real, with a different reality. And he was so unabashed and unrestrained.

Wasn't it rather horrible, a man who could be so soulful and spiritual, now to be so — she balked at her own thoughts and memories: then she added — so **bestial**? So **bestial**, they two! — so degraded! She winced. But after all, why not? She exulted as well. Why not be bestial, and go the whole round of experience? She exulted in it. She was bestial. How good it was to be really shameful! There would be no shameful thing she had not experienced. Yet she was unabashed, she was herself. Why not? She was free, when she knew everything, and no dark shameful things were denied her.

- One idea he clung to. Whatever he himself had done, Reed's daughter should not spend another night in that house of mysterious human and **bestial** inhabitants.
- 'That is no affair of yours,' I returned, for I was not going to indulge his **bestial** curiosity; 'it changes nothing in my present predicament.'

bilk [*bɪlk*]

Definition [*verb*]: Cheat somebody out of what is due, especially money
Definition [*verb*]: Hinder or prevent (the efforts, plans, or desires) of
Synonyms: thwart, queer, spoil, scotch, foil, cross, frustrate, baffle
Definition [*verb*]: Evade payment to
Definition [*verb*]: Escape, either physically or mentally
Synonyms: elude, evade
Examples:
- "She did not talk much, though she began by saying: 'Pay up at once, old man . . . You don't look like a fellow who would **bilk** a girl, but it puts me into better trim when I have been paid.'
- Mr. Johnson dropped his **bilk** hat upon the floor, and doubled up the hand which still clutched his kid gloves. He was very white. He scarcely knew the sound of his own voice.
- "And do you intend to make a secret of your going away?" said Jones. "I promise you," answered

Nightingale, "I don't intend to **bilk** my lodgings; but I have a private reason for not taking a formal leave."

- There is some dispute about land titles at Little **Bilk** Bar. About half a dozen cases were temporarily decided on Wednesday, but it is supposed the widows will renew the litigation. The only proper way to prevent these vexatious lawsuits is to hang the Judge of the County Court. Cow–County "Outcropper."
- Mr. Craw withdrew his chair, and the other lurched to his feet and came after him. The profanity of the drover, delivered in a hoarse roar, brought Mrs. Johnston back in alarm. The seller's case was far from clear, but it seemed to be his argument that Mr. Craw had taken delivery of a pup and was refusing payment. He was working himself into a fury at what he declared to be a case of strongly qualified **bilk**.

blatant [ˈbleɪtənt]

Definition [*adj*]: Without any attempt at concealment; completely obvious
Synonyms: blazing, conspicuous
Definition [*adj*]: Conspicuously and offensively loud; given to vehement outcry
Synonyms: clamant, clamorous, strident, vociferous
Examples:
- "Every reason in the world," he said, looking up at her with a bold, meaningful smile, that wanted to make its meaning **blatant**, if not patent.
- "Few had not, twenty years ago. He was one of the most 'blatant beasts' of the Reign of Terror. A fellow without honesty, conscience, or even common decency."
- "Oh, come off, now! Kipling! **Blatant** imperialist, anti-Stirner!" cried Carson Haggerty, kicking out each word with the assistance of his swinging left foot.
- The morning papers had featured the affair with **blatant** headlines. They had got my name. The Barbour & Hutchinson failure was resurrected.

bombast [ˈbambæst]

Definition [*noun*]: Pompous or pretentious talk or writing
Synonyms: fustian, rant, claptrap, blah
Examples:

- She was not yet quite seventeen. Not yet seventeen! the
  reader will say. She was still such a child, and yet
  arguing to herself about spendthrift debtors and self-
  sacrifice! All this **bombast** at sixteen and a half. No, my
  ungentle reader, not all this **bombast** at sixteen and a
  half. The **bombast** is mine. It is my fault if I cannot put
  into fitting language the thoughts which God put into her
  young heart. In her mind's soliloquy, Charley's vices
  were probably all summed up in the one word, unsteady.
  Why is he so unsteady? Why does he like these wicked
  things?' And then as regarded Mrs. Woodward, she did
  but make a resolve that not even for her love would she
  add to the unhappiness of that loving, tenderest mother.
  There was no bombast in Katie, either expressed or
  unexpressed.
- "Just so—but everyone who saw the letter would know
  that it was pretence and **bombast**. Of course you will do
  nothing of the kind."
- "Proceed," he begged, with a wave of his hand and a
  touch of his old **bombast**, which had collapsed so
  suddenly. "Proceed, I am all attention."
- You may also puzzle and bewilder your opponent by
  mere **bombast**; and the trick is possible, because a man
  generally supposes that there must be some meaning in
  words…

bourgeois [*bʊr'ʒwɑ*]

Definition [*noun*]: A capitalist who engages in industrial
commercial enterprise
Synonyms: businessperson
Definition [*noun*]: A member of the middle class
Synonyms: burgher
Definition [*adj*]: (according to Marxist thought) being of the
property-owning class and exploitive of the working class
Definition [*adj*]: Conforming to the standards and conventions of
the middle class
Synonyms: conservative, materialistic

Definition [*adj*]: Belonging to the middle class
Examples:

- And the abolition of this state of things is called by the **bourgeois**, abolition of individuality and freedom! And rightly so. The abolition of bourgeois individuality, bourgeois independence, and bourgeois freedom is undoubtedly aimed at.
- "**Bourgeois** law in relation to the distribution of the objects of consumption assumes, of course, inevitably a **bourgeois** state, for law is nothing without an apparatus capable of compelling observance of its norms. It follows (we are still quoting Lenin) that under Communism not only will **bourgeois** law survive for a certain time, but also even a **bourgeois** state without the **bourgeoisie**!"
- But don't wrangle with us so long as you apply, to our intended abolition of **bourgeois** property, the standard of your **bourgeois** notions of freedom, culture, law, etc. Your very ideas are but the outgrowth of the conditions of your **bourgeois** production and **bourgeois** property, just as your jurisprudence is but the will of your class made into a law for all, a will, whose essential character and direction are determined by the economical conditions of existence of your class.
- 'Bolshevism, it seems to me,' said Charlie, 'is just a superlative hatred of the thing they call the **bourgeois**; and what the **bourgeois** is, isn't quite defined. It is Capitalism, among other things. Feelings and emotions are also so decidedly **bourgeois** that you have to invent a man without them.
- By this, the long wished-for opportunity was offered to "True" Socialism of confronting the political movement with the Socialist demands, of hurling the traditional anathemas against liberalism, against representative government, against **bourgeois** competition, **bourgeois** freedom of the press, **bourgeois** legislation, **bourgeois** liberty and equality, and of preaching to the masses that they had nothing to gain, and everything to lose, by this **bourgeois** movement. German Socialism forgot, in the nick of time, that the French criticism, whose silly echo it was, presupposed the existence of modern **bourgeois** society, with its corresponding economic conditions of existence, and the political constitution adapted thereto,

the very things whose attainment was the object of the pending struggle in Germany.

burnish ['bɜrnɪʃ]

Definition [*noun*]: The property of being smooth and shiny
Synonyms: polish, gloss, glossiness
Definition [*verb*]: Polish and make shiny
Synonyms: buff, furbish
Examples:

- 'Tis well. At to-morrow's dawn my esquire shall begin to **burnish** up my armour — and caparison my courser. Till then adieu!
- "And I," said the landlord, after having watched the two gentlemen on their way to the Louvre, "I will go and **burnish** my sallet, put a match to my arquebuse, and sharpen my partisan, for no one knows what may happen."
- Before proceeding to the house of the lord, to whom I was to be offered, the mayor led me to a hotel, where we could make ourselves presentable to his excellency. Several servants, called maskatti, or dressers, joined us for this purpose. One took the mayor's sword to **burnish** it; another tied different colored bands to his tail. I will here remark, that nothing lays nearer to a monkey's heart than the adornment of his tail.
- Madame Desprez was an artist in the kitchen, and made coffee to a nicety. She had a knack of tidiness, with which she had infected the Doctor; everything was in its place; everything capable of polish shone gloriously; and dust was a thing banished from her empire. Aline, their single servant, had no other business in the world but to scour and **burnish**. So Doctor Desprez lived in his house like a fatted calf, warmed and cosseted to his heart's content.

buttress ['bətrɪs]

Definition [*noun*]: A support usually of stone or brick; supports the wall of a building
Synonyms: buttressing

Definition [*verb*]: Reinforce with a buttress
Definition [*verb*]: Make stronger or defensible
Examples:

- She paused beneath its shadow, for the stranger was close upon her. She saw him, oh, God! she saw him in that dim evening light. Her brain reeled, her heart stopped beating. She uttered no cry of surprise, no exclamation of terror, but staggered backward and clung for support to the ivied **buttress** of the archway. With her slender figure crouched into the angle formed by the buttress and the wall which it supported, she stood staring at the new-comer.
- "A bear;" cried Michael, who could not mistake the growling. "Nadia; Nadia!" And drawing his cutlass from his belt, Michael bounded round the **buttress** behind which the young girl had promised to wait.
- My eye always passes over the roofs filled with flowers, warbling, and sunlight, with the same pleasure; but to-day it stops at the end of a **buttress** which separates our house from the next.
- Satisfied with his scrutiny, he returned, despatched Abraham and Obadiah to the northwest corner of the church, placed Quilt behind a **buttress** near the porch, and sheltered himself behind one of the mighty elms.
- "Stand back, all of you," said Lee, "out of sight, behind that **buttress** a little way. Tell your mistress I want her," said he, to the servant who opened the door.

cabal [kəˈbæl]

Definition [*noun*]: A clique (often secret) that seeks power usually through intrigue
Synonyms: faction, junto, camarilla
Definition [*noun*]: A plot to carry out some harmful or illegal act (especially a political plot)
Synonyms: conspiracy
Definition [*verb*]: Engage in plotting or enter into a conspiracy, swear together
Synonyms: conspire, complot, conjure, machinate
Examples:

- "Why, then," said my father, "they may have the pleasure of **caballing** and cutting up one another, even in the same room."
- 'You are very unjust,' she said to him sobbing. 'I have never **caballed**. I have never done anything against you. Of course papa ought to know.'
- In what a confusion was the house! Princes, equerries, physicians, pages—all conferring, whispering, plotting, and **caballing**, how to induce the king to set off!
- During some years the word **Cabal** was popularly used as synonymous with Cabinet. But it happened by a whimsical coincidence that, in 1671, the Cabinet consisted of five persons the initial letters of whose names made up the word Cabal; Clifford, Arlington, Buckingham, Ashley, and Lauderdale. These ministers were therefore emphatically called the Cabal; and they soon made that appellation so infamous that it has never since their time been used except as a term of reproach.
- "Courtown, Courtown; powerful enough: but surely the good Viscount's skull is not exactly the head for the chief of a **cabal**?"

cajole [kə'dʒoʊl]

Definition [*verb*]: Influence or urge by gentle urging, caressing, or flattering
Synonyms: wheedle, palaver, blarney, coax, sweet-talk, inveigle
Examples:
- "Oh, mother!" he retorted superiorly. "Don't worry." And then, in a **cajoling** tone: "I've wanted to do that stag for ages."
- 'But, Mark, my dear fellow,' said Sowerby, trying to have recourse to the power of his **cajoling** voice. Robarts, however, would not listen.
- "Do you send a committee to a popular clergyman, and **cajole** him away from his congregation, by offering him a larger salary or greater perquisites?"
- 'Roy was busy, he was occupied. I won't have him abused. Besides, one can't be always caressing and **cajoling** one's pretty brats.'

- 'It's the first time,' he said, 'that I've ever been taken for a fox. Won't you sit down for a minute?' His voice was very soft and **cajoling**.

caulk [kɔk]

Definition [*noun*]: A waterproof filler and sealant that is used in building and repair to make watertight
Synonyms: caulking
Definition [*verb*]: Seal with caulking
Synonyms: calk
Examples:
- Cooktown is situated on the north side of a remarkably fine bay, at the mouth of the Endeavour River, and is surrounded by bold granite hills. The river received its name from Captain Cook's ship, the 'Endeavour,' which was beached here to **caulk** a leak. Mount Cook, as may be supposed, was named after the celebrated navigator himself.
- 'I stopped once, anchored for the night; oh, that's nothing of a sail with a fair wind. By Jove! I've forgotten to **caulk** that seam over your bunk, and it's going to rain. I must do it now. You turn in.'
- To save the reader trouble, I mention here, that the Hon. Kiffyn Fulke Verney has a habit of introducing the words "about it," as everybody is aware who has the honour of knowing him, without relation to their meaning, but simply to **caulk**, as it were, the seams of his sentences, to stop them where they open, and save his speech from foundering for want of this trifling half-pennyworth of oakum.
- "I told you you'd see life. Think o' the Pedantic now. Think o' her Number One chasin' the mobilised gobbies round the lower deck flats. Think o' the pore little snotties now bein' washed, fed, and taught, an' the yeoman o' signals with a pink eye wakin' bright 'an brisk to another perishin' day of five-flag hoists. Whereas we shall **caulk** an' smoke cigarettes, same as the Spanish destroyers did for three weeks after war was declared." He dropped into the wardroom singing…
- Florence had often wished to speak to this man; yet she had never taken courage to do so, as he made no

movement towards her. But one morning when she happened to come upon him suddenly, from a by-path among some pollard willows which terminated in the little shelving piece of stony ground that lay between his dwelling and the water, where he was bending over a fire he had made to **caulk** the old boat which was lying bottom upwards, close by, he raised his head at the sound of her footstep, and gave her Good morning.

censor [ˈsɛnsər]

Definition [*noun*]: Someone who censures or condemns
Definition [*noun*]: A person who is authorized to read publications or correspondence or to watch theatrical performances and suppress in whole or in part anything considered obscene or politically unacceptable
Definition [*verb*]: Forbid the public distribution of (a movie or a newspaper)
Synonyms: ban
Definition [*verb*]: Subject to political, religious, or moral censorship
Examples:

- After these remarks concerning the effects of the dream censor, let us now turn to their dynamics. I hope you will not consider the expression too anthropomorphically, and picture the dream censor as a severe little manikin who lives in a little brain chamber and there performs his duties; nor should you attempt to localize him too much, to think of a brain center from which his **censoring** influence emanates, and which would cease with the injury or extirpation of this center. For the present, the term "dream censor" is no more than a very convenient phrase for a dynamic relationship. This phrase does not prevent us from asking by what tendencies such influence is exerted and upon which tendencies it works; nor will we be surprised to discover that we have already encountered the dream censor before, perhaps without recognizing him.
- "That's the trouble with the American man. He really likes his sordid office. No, dearie, you just enjoy your leisure for a while yet. As soon as we finish the

campaign for **censoring** music you and I will run away and take a good trip — San Francisco and Honolulu."
- But from Scotland news seemed to come very slowly. Stephen's letters would quite often go unanswered; and what answers she received were unsatisfactory, for Angela's caution was a very strict **censor**. Stephen herself must write with great care, she discovered, in order to pacify that censor.

chauvinism [ˈʃoʊvəˌnɪzəm]

Definition [*noun*]: Overt sexism
Synonyms: Misogyny
Definition [*noun*]: Activity indicative of belief in the superiority of men over women
Synonyms: male chauvinism, antifeminism
Examples:
- "For my part I wish the excellent and gifted young man every success; I trust that youthful idealism and impulse towards the ideas of the people may never degenerate, as often happens, on the moral side into gloomy mysticism, and on the political into blind **chauvinism** — two elements which are even a greater menace to Russia than the premature decay, due to misunderstanding and gratuitous adoption of European ideas, from which his elder brother is suffering."
- The door to the conference room opened and closed tentatively. No one came out but Pat sat up and readied himself. Representing the fourth biggest industry in America, or almost representing it, he must not let a bunch of highbrows stare him down. He was not without an inside view of higher education — in his early youth he had once been the 'Buttons' in the DKE House at the University of Pennsylvania. And with encouraging **chauvinism** he assured himself that Pennsylvania had it over this pioneer enterprise like a tent.
- But the book, thanks to Ragaz, came out in good German. From Switzerland, it found its way, as early as December, 1914, to Austria and Germany. The Swiss Left-wingers F. Platten and others saw to that. Intended for German countries, the pamphlet was directed first of all against the German Social Democracy, the leading

party of the Second International. I remember that a journalist named Heilmann, who played first-violin in the orchestra of **chauvinism**, called my book mad, but quite logical in its madness. I could not have wished for greater praise. There was, of course, no lack of hints that my book was an artful tool of Entente propaganda.

- Otto Bauer and other Austrian Marxists privately admitted that Leitner, the foreign-news editor, had gone too far. In this they were simply echoing Adler himself, who, although he tolerated extremes of **chauvinism**, did not approve of them. But in the face of daring interference from outside, the leaders became united in sentiment. On one of the following Saturdays, Otto Bauer came up to the table at which Klyachko and I were sitting and began to rail at me. I confess that under his torrent of words I did not know what to say. I was astounded not so much by his lecturing tone as by the nature of his arguments.

- The French Socialist party was in a state of complete demoralization. There was no one to take the place Jaurés had left. Vaillant, the old "anti-militarist," was putting out daily articles in a spirit of intensest **chauvinism**. I once met the old man in the Committee of Action, which was made up of delegates of the party and the trade-unions. Vaillant looked like a shadow of himself — a shadow of Blanquism, with the traditions of sansculotte warfare, in an epoch of Raymond Poincaré. Pre-war France, with her arrested growth in population, her conservative economic life and thought, seemed to Vaillant the only country of progress or movement, the chosen, liberating nation whose contact alone awakens others to spiritual life. His socialism was **chauvinistic**, just as his **chauvinism** was messianic. Jules Guesde, the leader of the Marxist wing, who had exhausted himself in a long and trying struggle against the fetiches of democracy, proved to be capable only of laying down his untarnished moral authority on the "altar" of national defense.

coerce [kou'ɜrs]

Definition [*verb*]: To cause to do through pressure or necessity, by physical, moral or intellectual means: "She forced him to take a job in the city"
Synonyms: hale, squeeze, pressure, force
Examples:

- "Some one's been **coercing** him," thought Cheyne. "Now Constance would never have allowed that. Don't see as Europe could have done it any better."
- "Nature? Bah! I am no great believer in nature," gave back John, and emptied his glass of madeira. "Nature exists to be **coerced** and improved."
- I was never more surprised! Every word of it was surprising! My first words were: "but by what means are we to **coerce** and duly punish him?"
- Old Archibald Kane, keen, single-minded, of unsullied commercial honour, admired his son's determination, and did not attempt to **coerce** him.
- "Certainly it is a threat, as far as it goes. There is another threat which I may have to make for the sake of **coercing** you; but I do not wish to use it if I can do without it."

colossal [*kə'lasəl*]

Definition [*adj*]: So great in size or force or extent as to elicit awe
Synonyms: prodigious, stupendous
Examples:

- What was that? A light! A terrible light! Was it figures? Was it legs of a horse **colossal** — **colossal** above him: huge, huge?
- **Colossal** it certainly is, as Howells and Stedman agreed: **colossal** in its grotesqueness as in its sublimity. Howells, summarizing Mark Twain's gifts, has written.
- "That's **colossal**," said Parker, suddenly, striking the letter. "Never met anyone he could love. He'll never better that."
- 'A curious idea, though,' said Sullivan Smith, 'that some of the grand instructive figures were in their day **colossal** bores!'
- "The sleuth's all right, but the problem is **colossal**," Robert said. "The proverbial needle just gives itself up by comparison."

compassionate [kəm'pæʃənət]

Definition [*verb*]: Share the suffering of
Synonyms: feel for, pity, condole with, sympathize with
Definition [*adj*]: Showing or having compassion
Antonyms: uncompassionate
Examples:

- In the name of Allah the Compassionating, the **Compassionate**, we here indite, by the aidance of the Almighty and His furtherance, the History of the Caliph Harun Al-Rashid and of the Daughter of Kisra the King.
- In the mirror of the giltbordered pierglass the undecorated back of the dwarf tree regarded the upright back of the embalmed owl. Before the mirror the matrimonial gift of Alderman John Hooper with a clear melancholy wise bright motionless compassionate gaze regarded Bloom while Bloom with obscure tranquil profound motionless **compassionated** gaze regarded the matrimonial gift of Luke and Caroline Doyle.
- In the name of Allah, the **Compassionating**, the Compassionate, the Eternal One, the Termless, the Timeless, and of Him aidance we await. And here we begin (with the assistance of Allah Almighty and his fair furtherance) to invite the Story of Haykar the Sage, the Philosopher, the Wazir of Sankharib the Sovran, and of the son of the wise man's sister Nadan the Fool.
- "He's pulling off his wig!" whispered Gooseberry, **compassionating** my position, as the only person in the room who could see nothing.
- They were all in my sister's parlour adjoining: for I heard a confused mixture of voices, some louder than others, which drowned the more **compassionating** accents.

complement ['kamplɛmənt]

Definition [*noun*]: A word or phrase used to complete a grammatical construction
Definition [*noun*]: A complete number or quantity
Definition [*noun*]: Number needed to make up a whole force
Synonyms: full complement

Definition [*noun*]: Something added to complete or embellish or make perfect
Synonyms: accompaniment
Definition [*noun*]: One of a series of enzymes in the blood serum that are part of the immune response
Definition [*noun*]: Either of two parts that mutually complete each other
Definition [*verb*]: Make complete or perfect; supply what is wanting or form the complement to
Examples:

- The bourgeois family will vanish as a matter of course when its **complement** vanishes, and both will vanish with the vanishing of capital.
- Sir Philip then, with more than his usual **complement** of oaths, pronounced Miss Portman to be the finest girl he had ever seen, and took his leave.
- "A man like other men? — ay — that is to say, he has the usual **complement** of legs and arms, eyes and ears — But is he a sensible man?"
- Several irregularities follow, as the officers taking money to dismiss able seamen, and filling up their **complement** with raw and improper persons.
- "Shakespeare hadn't your overwhelming love of plastic beauty," I replied; "he fell in love with a dominant personality, the **complement** of his own yielding, amiable disposition."

culminate ['kəlmə,neɪt]

Definition [*verb*]: End, especially to reach a final or climactic stage
Synonyms: climax
Definition [*verb*]: Bring to a head or to the highest point
Definition [*verb*]: Reach the highest or most decisive point
Definition [*verb*]: Reach the highest altitude or the meridian, of a celestial body
Definition [*verb*]: Rise to, or form a summit
Examples:

- It was said, moreover, that the great wave of infidelity and mockery which was sweeping hourly over the country would **culminate** in a great riot to-morrow. . .

- "Thirdly, last and **culminating** article in this memorandum, we two agreed between ourselves that we love each other exclusively…"
- 'Such a shallow, cold, worldly, limited little brute!' said Bella, bringing out her last adjective with culminating force.
- "And in a world of men like this," Philip **culminated**, "we are waiting about for old Sempack's millennium to come of its own accord!"

curtail [ˈkɜrteɪ/]

Definition [*verb*]: Place restrictions on
Synonyms: restrict, curb, cut back
Definition [*verb*]: Terminate or abbreviate before its intended or proper end or its full extent
Synonyms: clip, cut short
Examples:
- 'But, Lady Camper, if I denude myself or **curtail** my income—a man at his wife's discretion, I was saying a man at his wife's mercy . . .!'
- "Mr. Trohm has no wish to intrude," was Mr. Gryce's conciliatory remark; but Mr. Trohm said nothing. He probably understood why Lucetta wished to **curtail** his stay in this house better than Mr. Gryce did.
- "If all the Fianna who have died in the last seven years were added to all that are now here," the stranger asserted, "I would treat all of these and those grievously, and would **curtail** their limbs and their lives."
- These bearings place the inner end of Thirsty Sound in latitude 22° 16'; and **curtail** the distance of thirty miles from Pier Head in captain Cook's chart, to twelve miles and a half.
- "Yes!" I replied. "You are going to London, and so am I. I have decided to **curtail** my visit by a few days, under the circumstances. I shall travel up with you. My luggage can follow."

demure [dɪˈmjʊr]

Definition [*adj*]: Affectedly modest or shy especially in a playful or provocative way
Synonyms: coy, overmodest
Examples:

- Finally, it was arranged that Larose should come in with them and receive a tenth share of any profit that was made. At first he **demured** a little at the smallness of his share, but in the end he agreed that it would do, at any rate to begin with.
- Hilda Bouverie glanced over her shoulder, but her employers had left the building. Her smile was less roguish than **demure**.
- It was but a sorry meal. The **demure** parlour-maid, as she handed the dishes and changed the plates, saw that all was not right, and was more demure than ever: neither father nor daughter could eat, and the hateful food was soon cleared away, and the bottle of port placed upon the table.
- 'And Herr Birchmore's daughter?' subjoined Christina, with a twinkle of mischief so **demure** that I could hardly be sure whether she meant it or not.
- "Well, you see, when I came down," she said again in that precise **demure** tone, "when I came down — into the garden Captain Anthony misunderstood."

denizen [ˈdɛnɪzən]

Definition [*noun*]: A person who inhabits a particular place
Synonyms: inhabitant, habitant, dweller, indweller
Definition [*noun*]: A plant or animal naturalized in a region
Examples:

- "He becomes very sentimental sometimes," explained Gatsby. "This is one of his sentimental days. He's quite a character around New York — a **denizen** of Broadway."
- A **denizen** is an alien born, but who has obtained ex donation regis [by royal gift] letters patent to make him an English subject: a high and incommunicable branch of the royal prerogative. A **denizen** is in a kind of middle state between an alien, and natural-born subject, and partakes of both of them. He may take lands by purchase or devise, which an alien may not; but cannot

take by inheritance: for his parent, through whom he must claim, being an alien had no inheritable blood, and therefore could convey none to the son. And, upon a like defect of hereditary blood, the issue of a **denizen**, born before denization, cannot inherit to him; but his issue born after, may. A **denizen** is not excused from paying the alien's duty, and some other mercantile burdens. And no denizen can be of the privy council, or either house of parliament, or have any office of trust, civil or military, or be capable of any grant from the crown.

- I would circle and perhaps wave a handkerchief, and then I meant to go over Lupton's gardens to the grounds of Sir Digby Foster. There a certain fair **denizen** might glance from the window . . .
- Kipling had written upon the card a compliment to me. This gave it an additional value in Susy's eyes, since, as a distinction, it was the next thing to being recognized by a **denizen** of the moon.
- The cries of the gorilla proclaimed that it was in mortal combat with some other **denizen** of the fierce wood. Suddenly these cries ceased, and the silence of death reigned throughout the jungle.

derogatory [dɪ'ragə,toʊri]

Definition [*adj*]: Expressive of low opinion
Synonyms: derogative, disparaging
Examples:
- "Yes, I repeat we have done nothing we need blush to avow, and nothing **derogatory** to our characters as Englishmen and gentlemen."
- 'Your ladyship must excuse me,' said I, with a noble air. 'During our present dispute respecting this house, I should deem it **derogatory** to my honour and my dignity, were I to enter it in the capacity of guest.'
- The example of Nausicaa, in the Odyssey, proves that the duties of the laundry were not thought **derogatory**, even from the dignity of a princess, in the heroic times.
- "More like a lot of women!" I thought to myself disgustedly, and then remembered how little like "women," in our **derogatory** sense, they were. She was smiling at me, reading my thought.

- Just the same, the morning after the enabling ordinances had passed, there was much **derogatory** comment in influential quarters. Mr. Norman Schryhart, who, through his publisher, had been fulminating defensively against Cowperwood, stared solemnly at Mr. Ricketts when they met.

disenfranchised [*dɪsɪnˈfræn,tʃaɪzd*]

Definition [*verb*]: Deprive of voting rights
Synonyms: disenfranchise, disfranchise
Antonyms: enfranchise
Definition [*adj*]: Deprived of the rights of citizenship especially the right to vote
Synonyms: disfranchised, voiceless, voteless
Antonyms: enfranchised
Examples:
- After this the day sagged. I fell to reckoning how long a man in a Turkish bath, weakened by excessive laughter, could live without food, and specially drink; and how long a **disenfranchised** bee could hold out under the same conditions.
- As computerization spreads across society, the populace at large is subjected to wave after wave of future shock. But, as a necessary converse, the "computer community" itself is subjected to wave after wave of incoming computer illiterates. How will those currently enjoying America's digital bounty regard, and treat, all this teeming refuse yearning to breathe free? Will the electronic frontier be another Land of Opportunity — or an armed and monitored enclave, where the **disenfranchised** snuggle on their cardboard at the locked doors of our houses of justice?
- And these changes were still going on. I became very emphatic for a time in these and other talks and writings, on the difference between "localized" and "delocalized" types of mind. I was quite sure I had come upon something important that had been previously overlooked. I had. Existing divisions, I argued, left everything in the hands of the "localized" types, and so long as we divided up our administrative areas on eighteenth century lines, the delocalized man with wider

interests and a wider range of movements, found himself virtually **disenfranchised** by his inability to attend intensively to the petty politics about his front door and garden. He might represent a strong body of opinion in the world, but he was in a minority in any particular constituency. We were in fact trying to modernize a world in which the modernized types were deprived of any influence.

- "I don't care a — for sides. What has my party done for me? Look at my cousin, Dick Morris. There's not a clergyman in Ireland stauncher to them than he has been, and now they've given the deanery of Kilfenora to a man that never had a father, though I condescended to ask for it for my cousin. Let them wait till I ask for anything again." Dr. Finn, who knew all about Dick Morris's debts, and who had heard of his modes of preaching, was not surprised at the decision of the Conservative bestower of Irish Church patronage; but on this subject he said nothing. "And as for George," continued the Earl, "I will never lift my hand again for him. His standing for Loughshane would be quite out of the question. My own tenants wouldn't vote for him if I were to ask them myself. Peter Blake" — Mr. Peter Blake was the lord's agent — "told me only a week ago that it would be useless. The whole thing is gone, and for my part I wish they'd disfranchise the borough. I wish they'd **disenfranchise** the whole country, and send us a military governor. What's the use of such members as we send? There isn't one gentleman among ten of them. Your son is welcome for me. What support I can give him he shall have, but it isn't much. I suppose he had better come and see me."

- Perhaps this is less than coincidence. Perhaps these two seemingly disparate worlds are somehow generating one another. The poor and **disenfranchised** take to the streets, while the rich and computer-equipped, safe in their bedrooms, chatter over their modems. Quite often the derelicts kick the glass out and break in to the lawyers' offices, if they see something they need or want badly enough. I cross the parking lot to the street behind the Attorney General's office. A pair of young tramps are bedding down on flattened sheets of cardboard, under an alcove stretching over the sidewalk. One tramp wears a glitter-covered T-shirt reading "CALIFORNIA" in Coca–Cola cursive. His nose and cheeks look chafed and swollen; they glisten with what seems to be Vaseline. The other tramp has a ragged long-sleeved shirt and lank brown hair parted in the middle. They both wear blue jeans coated in grime. They are both drunk. "You guys crash here a lot?" I ask them.

disobey [ˌdɪsəˈbeɪ]

Definition [*verb*]: Refuse to go along with; refuse to follow; be disobedient
Antonyms: obey
Examples:

- "Yes, sir, I hear." Fred had received this order before, and had secretly **disobeyed** it. He intended to **disobey** it again.
- "No circumstances, sir, can extenuate insubordination. I should be within my rights in sending you to the galleys. If out of several considerations I decline to do so, at least I cannot permit you to remain in Corfu. You disobeyed me once. You certainly shall have no chance of **disobeying** me again."
- "Good!" said the gendarme, placing his knee on his chest; "believe soft-spoken gentlemen again! Harkye, my friend, I have **disobeyed** my first order, but I will not disobey the second; and if you move, I will blow your brains out." And he levelled his carbine at Dantes, who felt the muzzle against his temple.
- Reason commands us far more imperiously than a master; for in **disobeying** the one we are unfortunate, and in disobeying the other we are fools.
- To commit a crime is to act against Divine justice — to **disobey** God. Therefore, as God cannot **disobey** Himself, He cannot commit crime; but He has so made man that man commits it frequently. How does that arise?

distraught [dɪˈstrɔt]

Definition [*adj*]: Deeply agitated especially from emotion

Synonyms: overwrought
Examples:

- He held out his hand and Enid stood hesitating and then retreated like one **distraught**; so distraught that she actually turned to Dr. Judson.
- Rachel put her arms round the tottering, **distraught** figure, drew it gently back into the room, and closed the door behind her.
- Presently Sa'id waxed weary of awaiting him and going forth in quest of him, found him walking in the garden, **distraught** and reciting these two couplets,
- The officer immediately ordered a canoe to receive M. d'Artagnan and himself. At sight of this he became almost **distraught** with rage.
- Ralph remained absent ten minutes. Raymon was **distraught**, ill at ease. He did not eat and kept looking at the door. At last the Englishman reappeared.

docile ['dɑsəl]

Definition [*adj*]: Willing to be taught or led or supervised or directed
Antonyms: stubborn
Definition [*adj*]: Ready and willing to be taught
Synonyms: teachable
Definition [*adj*]: Easily handled or managed
Synonyms: gentle
Examples:

- "It seems," replied the notary, "that young Michel, hitherto so gentle, and **docile**, and obedient, has fallen suddenly in love."
- Never had master a more anxious, humble, **docile** pupil. Never had pupil a more patient, unwearying, considerate, kindhearted master.
- The editor cannot always give his reasons; however strongly he may feel them, but the contributor, if sufficiently **docile**, can always divine them. It behooves him to be docile at all times, for this is merely the willingness to learn; and whether he learns that he is wrong, or that the editor is wrong, still he gains knowledge.

- Bertha waited for him, a prey to fresh anxiety. But, **docile** in everything, she would not go back to her friend till he returned.
- I seized this **docile** moment to propose our departure from the church. "First," she said, "let us replace the pavement above the vault."

dormant [ˈdɔrmənt]

Definition [*adj*]: In a condition of biological rest or suspended animation
Synonyms: hibernating, torpid
Definition [*adj*]: (of e.g. volcanos) not erupting and not extinct
Synonyms: inactive
Antonyms: active
Definition [*adj*]: Lying with head on paws as if sleeping
Synonyms: sleeping
Definition [*adj*]: Inactive but capable of becoming active
Synonyms: abeyant
Examples:
- "I suppose so. I suppose she had to. It isn't altogether a question of understanding; it's a question of living. With him, she was only half-alive; the rest was **dormant**, deadened. And the dormant woman was the femme incomprise, and she HAD to be awakened."
- "No rest, no business pleased my lovesick breast, my faculties became **dormant**, my mind torpid, and I lost my taste for poetry and song."
- Vance's **dormant** indignation against Bunty Hayes flamed up again. "Oh, he's the manager of 'Storecraft.' He was just doing a blurb for the show."
- "You mean somebody is so wicked that he has awakened a **dormant** moral sense even in a Bolshevist bookseller," said Pond. "Why, what has he done?"
- Roger Ferrison grinned. A sense of humour which had lain **dormant** in the backwoods of Canada was beginning to struggle up into the light.

dote [doʊt]

Definition [*verb*]: Be foolish or senile due to old age

Definition [*verb*]: Shower with love; show excessive affection for
Examples:
- The couple who dote upon their children have usually a great many of them: six or eight at least. The children are either the healthiest in all the world, or the most unfortunate in existence. In either case, they are equally the theme of their **doting** parents, and equally a source of mental anguish and irritation to their doting parents' friends.
- The Carrier had some faint idea of adding, 'dote upon you.' But, happening to meet the half-closed eye, as it twinkled upon him over the turned-up collar of the cape, which was within an ace of poking it out, he felt it such an unlikely part and parcel of anything to be **doted** on, that he substituted, 'that she don't believe it?'
- "Will you hold your silly tongue, my friend," said Santerre. "He is **doting**, quite doting, I see," and he turned round to his brother officers, as though appealing to them to corroborate his opinion.
- Her mother would have been concerned if she had known. Her mother **doted**. Her father would have been concerned too, for he also **doted**. Everybody **doted**. And when, melodiously obstinate, she had insisted on going off to entomb herself in Italy for a whole month with queer people she had got out of an advertisement, refusing even to take her maid, the only explanation her friends could imagine was that poor Scrap — such was her name among them — had overdone it and was feeling a little nervy.
- Mr. Pecksniff smiled through his tears, and slightly shook his head. 'You are very good,' he said, 'thank you. It is a great happiness to me, Mrs. Todgers, to make young people happy. The happiness of my pupils is my chief object. I **dote** upon 'em. They dote **upon** me too — sometimes.'

effigy ['ɛfɪdʒi]

Definition [*noun*]: A representation of a person (especially in the form of sculpture)
Synonyms: image, simulacrum
Examples:

- "Since you made Miss Bellingham's acquaintance, perhaps?" suggested Mr. Jellicoe, himself as unchanging in aspect as an Egyptian **effigy**.
- This **effigy** is in white marble, and represents the Knight in complete armor. Near him lies the effigy of his wife, and on her tomb is the following inscription; which, if really composed by her husband, places him quite above the intellectual level of Master Shallow.
- He had thrown off the seedy frockcoat, and now he was the Holmes of old in the mouse-coloured dressing-gown which he took from his **effigy**.
- "You look like the **effigy** of a young knight asleep on his tomb," she said, carefully tracing the well-cut profile defined against the dark stone.
- "She reminded me irresistibly of the **effigy** on the stone monument in Craymoor church, which Ella and I named "the wicked woman.""

effrontery [ɪˈfrəntərɪ]

Definition [*noun*]: Audacious (even arrogant) behavior that you have no right to
Synonyms: presumption, presumptuousness, assumption
Examples:
- An indescribable constraint, weariness, and humiliation were perceptible beneath this hardihood. **Effrontery** is a disgrace.
- Schryhart straightened up determinedly and offensively. This was outrageous, he thought, impossible! The effrontery of it!
- "And you really have the **effrontery** to tell me this," said she; "to tell me, who, as you very well know, set up to be a beauty myself, and who am at this very moment taking such an interest in your affairs, you really have the effrontery to tell me that Mrs. Bold is the most beautiful woman you know."
- "I believe Highlands and Lowlands ken that, sir, forby England and Holland," replied Ratcliffe, with the greatest composure and **effrontery**.
- But Miss Hyslup didn't hear anything after that first sentence. Miles, she was repeating to herself; Miles; the lady off the street had called her brother Miles. Wasn't

this something very strange, and unusual? Didn't it suggest either **effrontery**, or intimacy? No, no, not intimacy of course. But then — what **effrontery**!

emaciated [ɪˈmeɪʃiˌeɪtɪd]

Definition [*verb*]: Cause to grow thin or weak
Synonyms: waste, emaciate, macerate
Definition [*verb*]: Grow weak and thin or waste away physically
Definition [*adj*]: Very thin especially from disease or hunger or cold
Synonyms: bony, cadaverous, gaunt, haggard, pinched, skeletal, wasted
Examples:

- Those bodies which have been slowly **emaciated** should be slowly recruited; and those which have been quickly emaciated should be quickly recruited.
- "The pains of the body do not fatten a man," I said, "and the sufferings of the mind **emaciate** him. But we have suffered sufficiently, and we must be wise enough never to recall anything which can be painful to us."
- Then the Forestiers arrived, Madeleine looking charming in pink. Charles had become very much **emaciated** and coughed incessantly.
- An earnest-faced, **emaciated** man with a white moustache appealed to Bert. "Herr Booteraidge, sir, we are chust to start!"
- The **emaciated** appearance of the dying figure, the boy's thoughtless inattention, and the rapacious, unfeeling eagerness of the old nurse, are naturally and forcibly delineated.

emulate [ˈɛmjʊˌleɪt]

Definition [*verb*]: Strive to equal or match, especially by imitating
Definition [*verb*]: Imitate the function of (another system), as by modifying the hardware or the software
Definition [*verb*]: Compete with successfully; approach or reach equality with
Examples:

- Cease, then, **emulating** these paltry splitters of words, and emulate only the man of substance and honour, who is well to do.
- Mr. Barnes dropped the port, and Mrs. Barnes, **emulating** her daughter's example, screamed. The inspector, as though conscious of the draught, moved rapidly toward the window.
- The butler departed, and Titus, **emulating** Mr. Coates, who had already enveloped himself, like Juno at the approach of Ixion, in a cloud, proceeded to light his pipe.
- Thenceforth Italians were less concerned to outshine the glory of Garibaldi than to **emulate** the greater glory of Dante, Giotto and Galileo.
- The guests watched the movements of the captain silently and attentively, and, **emulating** his example, they also began to cross themselves, at which performance their caps and high hats flashed through the air like a flock of black birds.

enormous [ɪ'nɔrməs]

Definition [*adj*]: Extraordinarily large in size or extent or amount or power or degree; that a whole civilization should be dependent on technology"- Walter Lippman
Synonyms: tremendous
Examples:
- He pronounced the word **enormous** the second time with a jeering swell of the voice which might be tolerably well represented by capitals: "an **enormous**, ENORMOUS dog."
- "Schultze, I believe that is our clew!" he exclaimed keenly. "Certainly they would have been listed by the customs department; and come to think of it, the tariff on them would have been **enormous**, so **enormous** that— that——" and he lost the hopeful tone —"so **enormous** that we must have heard of it when it became a matter of public record."
- They are of course largely suggestive. The suggestive influence of environment plays an **enormous** part in all spiritual education.

- Two other patients next made their appearance, both of them **enormous**, and followed also by two attendants with naked arms.
- The flight of aeroplanes passed almost overhead followed by two **enormous** airships waddling along like monstrous sausages.

errant [ˈɛrənt]

Definition [*adj*]: Straying from the right course or from accepted standards
Definition [*adj*]: Uncontrolled motion that is irregular or unpredictable
Examples:
- "You took out the ink, Tom, when you was weighin' them oats today," said she, and out went Tom in search of that always **errant** and mitching article.
- "I don't know what to think," answered Sancho, "not being as well read as your worship in **errant** writings; but for all that I venture to say and swear that these apparitions that are about us are not quite Catholic."
- "Let him be the devil," said Gurth, "an he will. We can be no worse of waiting his return. If he belong to that party, he must already have given them the alarm, and it will avail nothing either to fight or fly. Besides, I have late experience, that **errant** thieves are not the worst men in the world to have to deal with."
- Barbon, who was ready to seek any port in the storm, and was already in the grip of Dougal's fierce vitality, wearily agreed. The pleasantness of the dinner had for a little banished his anxieties, but these had now returned and he foresaw a sleepless night. His thoughts turned naturally to his **errant** master.
- Mary tried to understand the hard, austere face, with its touch of cynicism. Conjecture as to its meaning was not difficult, but, in the utter absence of information, certainty there could be none. Under any circumstances, it was to be expected that Rhoda would think and speak of Mrs. Widdowson no less severely than of the **errant** Bella Royston.

exhilarating [ɪɡˈzɪlɜ-r,eɪtɪŋ]

Definition [*verb*]: Fill with sublime emotion
Synonyms: exhilarate, tickle pink, inebriate, thrill, exalt, beatify
Definition [*adj*]: Making lively and cheerful
Synonyms: stimulating
Definition [*adj*]: Making lively and joyful
Synonyms: elating
Examples:

- Helena's commended bowl to **exhilarate** the heart, had no other ingredient, as most of our critics conjecture, than this of borage.
- This was not an observation to **exhilarate** her spirits. She sighed: but Lionel, concluding himself the cause, begged her not to be low-spirited, but to write the letter at once.
- Howsoever you say, if this be true, that wine and strong drink have such virtue to expel fear and sorrow, and to **exhilarate** the mind, ever hereafter let's drink and be merry.
- "There's Mars — clear atmosphere, novel surroundings, **exhilarating** sense of lightness. It might be pleasant to go there."
- "That'll do now!" Babbitt flung in mechanically, as he lighted the gloriously satisfying first cigar of the day and tasted the **exhilarating** drug of the Advocate–Times headlines.

flout [flaʊt]

Definition [*verb*]: Treat with contemptuous disregard
Synonyms: scoff
Definition [*verb*]: Laugh at with contempt and derision
Synonyms: jeer, scoff, barrack, gibe
Examples:

- They stared at this novelty, resistance; and ere they could recover and make mincement of her, she put her pitcher quietly down, and threw her coarse apron over her head, and stood there grieving, her short-lived spirit oozing fast. "Hallo!" cried the soldier, "why, what is your ill?" She made no reply. But a little girl, who had long secretly hated the big ones, squeaked out, "They did **flout** her, they are aye **flouting** her; she may not come nigh the fountain for fear o' them, and 'tis a black shame."

- Moors and Jews sometimes place themselves under the protection of the foreign consuls, and then they can **flout** their riches in the Emperor's face with impunity.
- "To **flout** one's prince and insult one's superiors is the real rudeness," cried Mi Heng. "I bare my natural body as an emblem of my purity."
- "You are a rebel. You **flout** your Prince and injure your betters. The whole empire wishes to kill you. Do you think I am the only one?"
- "Oh, **flout** me not, and show your ill nature before the very soldier. In Heaven's name, what ill did I ever to ye? what harsh word cast back, for all you have flung on me, a desolate stranger in your cruel town, that ye **flout** me for my bereavement and my poor lad's most unwilling banishment? Hearts of flesh would surely pity us both, for that ye cast in my teeth these many days, ye brows of brass, ye bosoms of stone."

forebode [*four'boud*]

Definition [*verb*]: Make a prediction about; tell in advance
Synonyms: predict, foretell, prognosticate, call, anticipate, promise
Examples:

- Madeline Whitmarsh herself opened the door. She took them down the long-flagged hall to the dining-room, a cheerful enough apartment whatever its exterior might **forebode**.
- Meanwhile Leona, whose ears the manager's speech was not intended to reach, stood apart, thoughtful and anxious, wondering whether the whispered conversation **foreboded** good or evil to her.
- It might have been worse, replied my uncle Toby. — I don't comprehend, said my father. — Suppose the hip had presented, replied my uncle Toby, as Dr. Slop **foreboded**.
- "Barbara, I say, don't you think this dream, coming uncalled for uninduced, must **forebode** some ill? Rely

upon it, something connected with that wretched murder is going to be stirred up again."

- "I thought so once; I doubt now — yet, in doubting, hope. But why do you alarm me with these questions? You, too, **forebode** that in this visit I may lose her forever?"

gaudiness ['gɔdinɛs]

Definition [*noun*]: Tasteless showiness
Synonyms: flashiness, garishness, loudness, brashness, meretriciousness, tawdriness, glitz
Definition [*noun*]: Strident color or excessive ornamentation
Synonyms: garishness
Examples:

- The little woman stood a moment pensive and then sighed. Joseph caressed his nose, a nose which for **gaudiness** could vie with any floral display.
- Hers, after all, was an ideal existence. She had plenty to eat, as much tobacco as was good for her, and outer raiment that in **gaudiness** outrivalled the flame-tree and the yellow hibiscus. She was the favourite of two consorts, and only when her pride and scorpion-like attributes got the better of her was she corrected.
- He had explained that, in preference to the **gaudiness** of Palm Beach and Miami, he had chosen a plain West Coast Florida resort, for privacy, for adventurous fishing, for bathing and shell-hunting on great lonely beaches. He had never seen the place, but Harley Bozard said the food was excellent and the fishing superb. She'd certainly enjoy catching a tarpon.
- He wore for the ceremony a new double-breasted suit of black broadcloth, and new black shoes. So did Eddie Fislinger, along with a funereal tie and a black wide felt hat, like a Texas congressman's. But Elmer was more daring. Had he not understood that he must show dignity, he would have indulged himself in the **gaudiness** for which he had a talent. He had compromised by buying a beautiful light gray felt hat in Chicago, on his way home, and he had ventured on a red-bordered gray silk handkerchief, which gave a pleasing touch of color to his sober chest.

- The Palace of Lachen was at this moment wholly uninhabited, and shown to us by some common servant. It is situated in a delicious park d'Anglaise, and with a taste, a polish, and an elegance that clears it from the charge of frippery or **gaudiness**, though its ornaments and embellishments are all of the liveliest gaiety. There is in some of the apartments some Gobelin tapestry, of which there are here and there parts and details so exquisitely worked that I could have "hung over them enamoured."

glean [*glin*]

Definition [*verb*]: Gather, as of natural products
Synonyms: reap, harvest
Examples:
- And when she was risen up to **glean**, Boaz commanded his young men, saying, let her glean even among the sheaves, and reproach her not.
- If grapegatherers come to thee, would they not leave some **gleaning** grapes? if thieves by night, they will destroy till they have enough.
- "Oh, it's straight enough — more than she is!" retorted her husband, who was slightly jealous of having his facts reinforced by any information not of his own **gleaning**.
- This was not a very satisfactory result. Davidson stayed on, and even joined the table d'hote dinner, without **gleaning** any more information. He was resigned.
- And, nodding pleasantly to Marechal, Mademoiselle Herzog joined her father, who was **gleaning** details about the house of Desvarennes from Savinien.

impair [*æN_'pɛR*]

Definition [*verb*]: Make worse or less effective
Definition [*verb*]: Make imperfect
Synonyms: mar, spoil, deflower, vitiate
Examples:
- And further, should one child (and there are three) require a pair of shoes, the family must strike meat for a week from its bill of fare. And since there are five pairs of

feet requiring shoes, and five heads requiring hats, and five bodies requiring clothes, and since there are laws regulating indecency, the family must constantly impair its physical efficiency in order to keep warm and out of jail. For notice, when rent, coals, oil, soap, and firewood are extracted from the weekly income, there remains a daily allowance for food of 4.5d. to each person; and that 4.5d. cannot be lessened by buying clothes without **impairing** the physical efficiency.

- "Twelve years!" rejoined Harding. "Ah! Twelve years of solitude, after a wicked life, perhaps, may well **impair** a man's reason!"
- 'Up with you,' said the stranger, assisting Mr. Pickwick on to the roof with so much precipitation as to **impair** the gravity of that gentleman's deportment very materially.
- "Miss Dare," said he, in his slow, kindly way that nothing could **impair**, "do you realize the nature of the evidence you have given to the court?"
- "But why don't you smoke — come. You don't think that tobacco, when in league with wine, too much enhances the latter's vinous quality — in short, with certain constitutions tends to **impair** self-possession, do you?"

imperious [ɪmˈpiriəs]

Definition [*adj*]: Having or showing arrogant superiority to and disdain of those one views as unworthy
Synonyms: disdainful, haughty, lordly, overbearing, prideful, sniffy, supercilious, swaggering
Examples:
- The threat was extravagant; but Youth's glowing cheek and eye, and **imperious** lip, and simple generosity, made it almost beautiful.
- This **imperious** signal drew her to another attempt. The deplorable sound that came sent Emilia sinking down with a groan.
- Footsteps were heard in the corridor, and instantly the **imperious** detective was merged back into the obsequious workman.
- Cigarette sprang to her feet, vivacious, **imperious**, reckless, dared to anything by the mere fact of being publicly arraigned.

- "Stay where you are," cried the hag, in an **imperious** tone. "I want to speak to you. Come nearer to me, my pretty wheans; nearer—nearer."

impregnable [ɪmˈprɛgnəbəl]

Definition [*adj*]: Immune to attack; incapable of being tampered with
Synonyms: inviolable, secure, strong, unassailable, unattackable
Definition [*adj*]: Capable of conceiving
Synonyms: conceptive
Definition [*adj*]: Incapable of being overcome, challenged or refuted
Synonyms: inexpugnable
Examples:
- Recalling Moore's **impregnable** good humor under Nils' own attacks, I began to wonder exactly what was the latter's object.
- "Neither your musketeers, nor your whole army could take Belle–Isle," said Fouquet, coldly. "Belle–Isle is **impregnable**."
- "Let us be back'd with God and with the seas Which He hath given for fence **impregnable**, and with their helps alone defend ourselves."
- He led stormers against well-nigh **impregnable** forts, and died on the ramparts at the moment of victory. (His grave was watered by a nation's tears.)
- "Don't apologise. We are not plighted yet, and that **impregnable** air of Mrs. Bosworth may keep me off as well as her other lovers."

inadvertent [ˌɪnədˈvɜrtənt]

Definition [*adj*]: Happening by chance or unexpectedly or unintentionally
Synonyms: accidental
Examples:
- All eyes were turned on the young fellow's face in surprise and reprehension; and he uneasily attempted to carry off his **inadvertent** solecism with a sort of swagger.

- "Ah! Wretched princess!" cried Isabella; "what hast thou done! what ruin has thy **inadvertent** goodness been preparing for thyself, for me, and for Matilda!"
- When in an **inadvertent** moment I said that certain sects had believed in infant damnation — and explained it — she sat very still indeed.
- "And so they are, Abel Crew," rejoined Cathy, emphatically. "The week before last, which I was spending at home at father's, I changed the one pill-box for the other, **inadvertent**, you see"— with a nod to the coroner — "and took the wrong box away with me. And I wish both boxes had been in the sea before I'd done it."
- Swithin could not sleep that night for thinking of his Viviette. Nothing told so significantly of the conduct of her first husband towards the poor lady as the abiding dread of him which was revealed in her by any sudden revival of his image or memory. But for that consideration her almost childlike terror at Swithin's inadvertent disguise would have been ludicrous.

invidious [ɪnˈvɪdiəs]

Definition [*adj*]: Containing or implying a slight or showing prejudice
Synonyms: discriminatory
Examples:
- 'I didn't make use of the word in any **invidious** sense, ma'am,' replied Mr. Benjamin Allen, growing somewhat uneasy on his own account.
- "He's there — he's there!" she declared once more as she made, on the child, with an almost **invidious** tug, a strained undergarment "meet."
- "Yes, Morris," said the girl, with her imagination — what there was of it — swimming in this happy truth, which seemed, after all, **invidious** to no one.
- "Nay, I can give you no reason to the contrary; but in your place I should not much regret losing the chance of such precarious and **invidious** elevation."

irascible [aɪˈræsəbəl]

Definition [*adj*]: Quickly aroused to anger
Synonyms: choleric, hotheaded, hot-tempered, quick-tempered, short-tempered
Definition [*adj*]: Characterized by anger
Synonyms: choleric
Examples:

- "But do you see, Professor," replied our **irascible** companion, "that we shall absolutely die of hunger in this iron cage?"
- He had to deal with holly bushes, nettles, hawthorns, eglantines, thistles, and very **irascible** brambles. He was much lacerated.
- Jim watched the dark, **irascible** little man with amusement. They rose, and went to look for an inn, and beer. Tanny still clung rather stickily to Jim's side.
- 'Shut up!' resumed a comrade, a very **irascible** little painter with a fair complexion. 'You surely don't want to make us swallow such a turnip as that?'
- Mr. George sits squared in exactly the same attitude, looks at the painted ceiling, and says never a word. The **irascible** Mr. Smallweed scratches the air.

irrefutable [ɪˈrɛfjətəbəl]

Definition [*adj*]: Impossible to deny or disprove
Synonyms: incontrovertible, positive
Examples:

- "We shall have certain, **irrefutable**, convincing, and infallible proof," replied Ferguson, "should the wind hold another hour in our favor!"
- The theory seems **irrefutable** just because the act of transference of the people's will cannot be verified, for it never occurred.
- The fact, however, is **irrefutable** that dream-formation is based on a process of condensation. How, then, is this condensation effected?
- 'Well done, Davies,' I thought. He had told his story well, using no subtlety. I knew it was exactly how he would have told it to anyone else, if he had not had **irrefutable** proof of foul play.
- Lecoq had already noted this circumstance, which seemed to furnish an **irrefutable** argument in favor of

the assertions made by the landlady and the prisoner. "Are you sure," he asked, "that this is the man's handwriting?"

juxtaposed [ˌdʒʌkstʌˈpoʊzd]

Definition [*verb*]: Place side by side
Synonyms: juxtapose
Definition [*adj*]: Placed side by side often for comparison
Examples:
- But even a woman cannot live only into the distance, the beyond. Willy-nilly she finds herself **juxtaposed** to the near things, the thing in itself. And willy-nilly she is caught up into the fight with the immediate object.
- The opposite verdicts passed upon his work by his contemporaries bear witness to the extraordinary mingling of defects and merits in his mental character. Here are a few, **juxtaposed**...
- On this account, those of which we speak must have been of the earliest in date, since without them the defense of the organism would have been impossible. From the time when the cellules were no longer merely **juxtaposed**, but were called upon to give mutual aid, it was needful that a mechanism organize analogous to what we have described, so that this aid miss not its way, but forestall the peril.
- The sight of these antique fragments disgusted Daisy; they littered the path, and she could not imagine them built up into a rockery that should have the smallest claim to be an attractive object. How could the **juxtaposition** of a stone mullion, a drain-pipe and an ammonite present a pleasant appearance? Besides, who was to **juxtapose** them? She could not keep pace with the other needs of the garden, let alone a rockery, and where, after all, was the rockery to stand? The asparagus-bed seemed the only place, and she preferred asparagus.
- He might have searched Europe over for a greater contrast between **juxtaposed** scenes. The spectacle was that of the eighth chasm of the Inferno as to colour and flame, and, as to mirth, a development of the Homeric heaven. A smoky glare, of the complexion of

brass-filings, ascended from the fiery tongues of innumerable naphtha lamps affixed to booths, stalls, and other temporary erections which crowded the spacious market-square. In front of this irradiation scores of human figures, more or less in profile, were darting athwart and across, up, down, and around, like gnats against a sunset.

laborious [lə'boʊriəs]

Definition [adj]: Characterized by effort to the point of exhaustion; especially physical effort
Synonyms: arduous, backbreaking, grueling, hard, heavy, operose, punishing, toilsome
Examples:
- It is the fancy that swells your milliner's bill, the newly-invented trimmings, the complex and **laborious** combinations."
- Through learned and **laborious** years they set themselves to find Fresh terrors and undreamed-of fears to heap upon mankind.
- "We could not find any one there," Mr. Billingham continued, speaking with **laborious** care. "We hoped there was nothing wrong."
- See the **laborious** history of Ducange, whose accurate table of the French dynasties recapitulates the thirty-five passages, in which he mentions the dukes of Athens.
- The irony of this **laborious** period was full of self-pity. His voice quavered at the close, and a tremor was noticeable in his stiff frame.

latent ['leɪtənt]

Definition [adj]: Potentially existing but not presently evident or realized
Definition [adj]: (pathology) not presently active
Examples:
- The first process of the dream-work is condensation. By this we understand that the manifest dream has a smaller content than the **latent** one, that is, it is a sort of abbreviated translation of the latter. Condensation may

occasionally be absent, but as a rule it is present, often to a very high degree. The opposite is never true, that is, it never occurs that the manifest dream is more extensive in scope and content than the **latent**. Condensation occurs in the following ways: 1. Certain **latent** elements are entirely omitted; 2. only a fragment of the many complexes of the **latent** dream is carried over into the manifest dream; 3. **latent** elements that have something in common are collected for the manifest dream and are fused into a whole.

- "As a rule a hypnotic subject can be influenced by the operator only, but your daughter's is a peculiar case; she is super-sensitive. I think it possible that she might be influenced by anybody in whom the hypnotic power was either **latent** or developed. I have no doubt that it is **latent** in you."

- The consequence of condensation for the relation between **latent** and manifest dreams is the fact that no simple relations can exist between the elements of the one and the other. A manifest element corresponds simultaneously to several **latent** ones, and vice versa, a **latent** element may partake of several manifest ones, an interlacing, as it were. In the interpretation of the dream it also becomes evident that the associations to a single element do not necessarily follow one another in orderly sequence. Often we must wait until the entire dream is interpreted.

- 'Do you?' said Miss Grandison. 'Well, I have sometimes thought that you might have a **latent** suspicion of that subject, too. I thought you were his confidant.'

- The **latent** ink rushes into being at the contact of those few drops. The whole cup is black with it, transfused with impenetrable darkness, terrible to look upon.

lethargic [lə'θardʒɪk]

Definition [*adj*]: Deficient in alertness or activity
Synonyms: unenergetic
Antonyms: energetic
Examples:

- At that moment, Marius slowly opened his eyes, and his glance, still dimmed by **lethargic** wonder, rested on M. Gillenormand.
- The Prince replied with a word which sounded to Jaikie like "Unnutz," a word which woke a momentary interest in his **lethargic** mind.
- A massive and **lethargic** woman, who had been urging Daisy to play golf with her at the local club to-morrow, spoke in Miss Baedeker's defense…
- "Only! My dear, good lady, this perpetual, stupid, **lethargic** sleepiness is not natural. You are young, perhaps inexperienced, or you would know it to be not so."
- By his frequent and soothing interpolation of the word "just" he aroused her **lethargic** enthusiasm. Strutting violently about the room, he simulated a dynamic and irresistible efficiency. "We'll buy a car to-morrow."

lien ['laɪən]

Definition [*noun*]: The right to take another's property if an obligation is not discharged
Definition [*noun*]: A large dark-red oval organ on the left side of the body between the stomach and the diaphragm; produces cells involved in immune responses
Synonyms: spleen
Examples:
- Though ye have **lien** among the pots, yet shall ye be as the wings of a dove covered with silver, and her feathers with yellow gold.
- "That's what I call having a **lien** upon a daughter's property," cried the notary. "Make her look her best to-night," he added with a sly glance.
- And Abimelech said, What is this thou hast done unto us? one of the people might lightly have **lien** with thy wife, and thou shouldest have brought guiltiness upon us.
- The two pages that Wiese wrote at Henry's dictation relinquished all **lien** on the children thence and forever for himself and Choupette. When they had affixed trembling signatures Wiese cried…

- Amherst smiled. "That sounds very young — if you'll excuse my saying so. Well, I won't go on to insinuate that, Truscomb being high in favour with the Westmores, and the Westmores having a **lien** on the hospital, Disbrow's position there is also bound up with his taking — more or less — the same view as Truscomb's."

loll [/*lɑl*/]

Definition [*verb*]: Hang loosely or laxly
Synonyms: droop
Definition [*verb*]: Be lazy or idle
Synonyms: bum, bum around, bum about, loaf, waste one's time, lounge around, lounge about
Examples:
- I took the swivel, and aimed coolly. **Loll** Mahommed, his palanquin, and his men, were now not above two hundred yards from the fort. Loll was straight before me, gesticulating and shouting to his men. I fired — bang!!!
- What a thing is luck! If **Loll** Mahommed had not been made to take that ride round the camp, I should infallibly have been lost.
- "It's Sibyl!" she said with a half-laughing half-apologetic flash of her brown eyes at us all — "I never can loll before Sibyl!"

malevolent [*mə'lɛvələnt*]

Definition [*adj*]: Wishing or appearing to wish evil to others; arising from intense ill will or hatred
Definition [*adj*]: Having or exerting a malignant influence
Synonyms: malefic, malign, evil
Examples:
- Without waiting for a reply, but darting a **malevolent** look at the prisoner, he quitted the cell, the door of which was instantly double-locked and bolted.
- "Therefore," drawled the **malevolent**, "you are answerable for all the mischief he does with it, and mischief assuredly he will do."

- "There, Orrin," I broke in, "you do him wrong. The Colonel is above your comprehension as he is above mine; but there is nothing **malevolent** in him."
- 'There!' sang Hermione, with a strange ring of **malevolent** victory. 'I'm so sorry, so awfully sorry. Can't you get it, Gerald?'
- Ghosts being seldom dangerous to human life, we follow up the homicidal Glam with a Scottish traditional story of **malevolent** and murderous sprites.

mendacious [mɛnˈdeɪʃəs]

Definition [*adj*]: Given to lying
Definition [*adj*]: Intentionally untrue
Examples:
- "Church?" answered I, "that is a kind of state, and indeed the most **mendacious**. But remain quiet, thou dissembling dog! Thou surely knowest thine own species best!
- "I am an old man and fear not death," answered Babalatchi, with a **mendacious** assumption of indifference. "But what will you do?"
- **Mendacious** Mr. Wrenn! As we have commented. He put his head on one side, rubbed his chin with nice consideration, and condescended, "What would you suggest?"
- At which Stephen must blush and grow slightly **mendacious**, pretending to give all the credit to the pony, pretending to feel very humble of spirit, which she knew she was far from feeling.
- 'Then everything he told me last night, I suppose, was **mendacious**: he delivered himself of a series of the stiffest statements. They stuck, when I tried to swallow them, but I never thought of so simple an explanation.'

mystique [mɪˈstik]

Definition [*noun*]: An aura of heightened value or interest or meaning surrounding a person or thing
Examples:

- Here we reach the central secret. As we have seen. the **mystique** of the Party, and above all of the Inner Party, depends upon DOUBLETHINK But deeper than this lies the original motive, the never-questioned instinct that first led to the seizure of power and brought DOUBLETHINK, the Thought Police, continuous warfare, and all the other necessary paraphernalia into existence afterwards. This motive really consists . . .
- In Aldous Huxley's Brave New World, a sort of post-war parody of the Wellsian Utopia, these tendencies are immensely exaggerated. Here the hedonistic principle is pushed to its utmost, the whole world has turned into a Riviera hotel. But though Brave New World was a brilliant caricature of the present (the present of 1930), it probably casts no light on the future. No society of that kind would last more than a couple of generations, because a ruling class which thought principally in terms of a "good time" would soon lose its vitality. A ruling class has got to have a strict morality, a quasi-religious belief in itself, a **mystique**. London was aware of this, and though he describes the caste of plutocrats who rule the world for seven centuries as inhuman monsters, he does not describe them as idlers or sensualists. They can only maintain their position while they honestly believe that civilization depends on themselves alone, and therefore in a different way they are just as brave, able and devoted as the revolutionaries who oppose them.
- All the beliefs, habits, tastes, emotions, mental attitudes that characterize our time are really designed to sustain the **mystique** of the Party and prevent the true nature of present-day society from being perceived. Physical rebellion, or any preliminary move towards rebellion, is at present not possible. From the proletarians nothing is to be feared. Left to themselves, they will continue from generation to generation and from century to century, working, breeding, and dying, not only without any impulse to rebel, but without the power of grasping that the world could be other than it is. They could only become dangerous if the advance of industrial technique made it necessary to educate them more highly; but, since military and commercial rivalry are no longer important, the level of popular education is actually

declining. What opinions the masses hold, or do not hold, is looked on as a matter of indifference. They can be granted intellectual liberty because they have no intellect. In a Party member, on the other hand, not even the smallest deviation of opinion on the most unimportant subject can be tolerated.

nebulous ['nɛbjələs]

Definition [*adj*]: Lacking definite form or limits
Synonyms: cloudy, nebulose
Definition [*adj*]: Of or relating to or resembling a nebula
Synonyms: nebular
Definition [*adj*]: Lacking definition or definite content
Synonyms: unfixed
Examples:
- And behold! In the southward, low down and glittering swiftly nearer, were two little patches of **nebulous** light. And then two more, and then a **nebulous** glow of swiftly driving shapes. Presently he could count them. There were four and twenty. The first fleet of aeroplanes had come! Beyond appeared a yet greater glow.
- 'The usual type nowadays,' St. Peter returned. 'A young Power in charge of some half-baked Universe. Never having dealt with life yet, he's somewhat **nebulous**.'
- Mrs. Toplady's voice died away in a considerate vagueness. But May was not at all disposed to leave the matter **nebulous**.
- Kenton followed the pointing finger. A mighty mass loomed darkly in the silvery haze, its **nebulous** outlines cone-shaped, its top flattened. His heart quickened.
- Then comes the question, What is the policy of Socialism? If Toryism and Democracy are only **nebulous** masses of opposition to the solid centre of Whiggery, what can we call Socialism?

nettle ['nɛtəl]

Definition [*noun*]: Any of numerous plants having stinging hairs that cause skin irritation on contact (especially of the genus Urtica or family Urticaceae)

Definition [*verb*]: Sting with or as with nettles and cause a stinging pain or sensation
Synonyms: urticate
Definition [*verb*]: Cause annoyance in; disturb, especially by minor irritations
Synonyms: annoy, rag, get to, bother, get at, irritate, rile, nark, gravel, vex, chafe, devil
Examples:

- "Oh, nettle-plant, Little nettle-plant, What dost thou here alone? I have known the time When I ate thee unboiled, When I ate thee unroasted."
- He began to reason interminably with himself. Why, after all, was he seized? Caterham had been in office two days — just long enough — to grasp his **Nettle**! Grasp his Nettle! Grasp his Giant Nettle! The refrain once started, sang through his mind, and would not be dismissed.
- "To which nettle-plant?" asked she; "I don't talk to nettle-plants." "If thou didst not do it, then thou art not the true bride," said he. So she bethought herself, and said,
- A boy was stung by a **Nettle**. He ran home and told his Mother, saying, "Although it hurts me very much, I only touched it gently." "That was just why it stung you," said his Mother. "The next time you touch a Nettle, grasp it boldly, and it will be soft as silk to your hand, and not in the least hurt you."
- At the same time, out of the squalid world sometimes would come a rank, evil smell of selfishness and degraded lust, the smell of that awful **nettle**, She-who-was-Cynthia. This nettle actually contrived, at intervals, to get a little note through to her girls, her children. And at this the silver-haired Mater shook inwardly with hate. For if She-who-was-Cynthia ever came back, there wouldn't be much left of the Mater. A secret gust of hate went from the old granny to the girls, children of that foul nettle of lust, that Cynthia who had had such an affectionate contempt for the Mater.

objurgate [ˈɑbdʒərˌgeɪt]

Definition [*verb*]: Express strong disapproval of
Synonyms: condemn, reprobate, decry, excoriate

Definition [*verb*]: Censure severely
Synonyms: chastise, castigate, chasten, correct
Examples:

- 'Prayers!' He was about to **objurgate**, but affirmatived her motion to ring the bell for the servants, and addressed Peterborough: 'You read 'em abroad every morning?'
- To all which our poor Legislative, tied up by an unmarching Constitution, can oppose nothing, by way of remedy, but mere bursts of parliamentary eloquence! They go on, debating, denouncing, **objurgating**: loud weltering Chaos, which devours itself.
- With the loose end of bark in his bill, tugging and fluttering, using his tail as a lever with the tree as a fulcrum, and **objurgating** in unseemly tones, as the bark resists his efforts, the drongo assists the Moreton Bay ash in discarding worn-out epidermis, and the tree reciprocates by offering safe nesting-place on its most brittle branches.
- Based on the uncompromising manner the Arabs present their demands, one might assume that they won the war, not Israel. They precipitate a conflict, make explicit demands of the victor and threaten another Intifada unless Israel complies with their ultimatums. Instead of being criticized for their intransigence, Arab **objurgate** directives are viewed as totally reasonable.
- Veto after Veto; your thumbscrew paralysed! Gods and men may see that the Legislative is in a false position. As, alas, who is in a true one? Voices already murmur for a 'National Convention.' (December 1791 (Hist. Parl. xii. 257).) This poor Legislative, spurred and stung into action by a whole France and a whole Europe, cannot act; can only **objurgate** and perorate; with stormy 'motions,' and motion in which is no way: with effervescence, with noise and fuliginous fury!

oscillate ['ɑsə,leɪt]

Definition [*verb*]: Be undecided about something; waver between conflicting positions or courses of action
Synonyms: hover, vibrate, vacillate
Definition [*verb*]: Move or swing from side to side regularly

Synonyms: vibrate
Examples:

- 'It was later still that I discovered still another thing. Each of those great vague mounds had begun to **oscillate** as it circled round about us. I was conscious at the same time that there was communicated to the vessel the beginning of a similar **oscillating** movement, so very slight at first that I could scarcely be sure she so much as moved.
- "Oh, only the winter. I am a vagrant really: or a migrant. I must migrate. Do you think a cuckoo in Africa and a cuckoo in Essex is one AND the same bird? Anyhow, I know I must **oscillate** between north and south, so oscillate I do. It's just my nature. All people don't have the same needs."
- Chimeras! The charm had vanished which had once caused the love of Martial de Sairmeuse to **oscillate** between Mlle. de Courtornieu and the daughter of Lacheneur.
- Between the horror of returning once again, and the horror of the step into another darkness, his soul **oscillated** with the feeble violence of despair.
- A shuddering passed through the crowding cones. I saw the tremor shake their bristling hosts, **oscillate** the great spire, set the faceted disks quivering.

ostentatious [ˌastʌnˈteɪʃʌs]

Definition [*adj*]: Intended to attract notice and impress others
Synonyms: pretentious
Antonyms: unostentatious
Definition [*adj*]: (of a display) tawdry or vulgar
Synonyms: pretentious
Examples:

- "The Oriental peoples didn't have an Age of Chivalry. They didn't need one," Lillian observed. "And this reserve — it becomes in itself **ostentatious**, a vain-glorious vanity."
- Dr. Oldacre, new come from church, with an **ostentatious** Prayer-book in his kid-gloved hand, broke in upon his meditation.

- "That's what I want to know," whined the person in sequins, who had contributed various ejaculations unworthy of report, and finally subsided behind an **ostentatious** fan.
- Her plain purple coat and wide Leghorn hat, with black ribbons, had the effect not of elegance, but of insignificance. Susannah thought it **ostentatious**, too.
- The Inspector looked blank; but a light dawned gradually on the face of the priest, who said at last with almost **ostentatious** unconcern.

parochial [pə'roʊkiəl]

Definition [*adj*]: Relating to or supported by or located in a parish
Definition [*adj*]: Narrowly restricted in outlook or scope
Synonyms: insular
Examples:
- Denis McGovery now hurried off. Father John called for Judy to take away the cold tea, and prepared to sally forth to some of his numerous **parochial** duties.
- The conversation drifted not unnaturally from **parochial** to more personal topics, and Mr. Jardine showed himself interested in Bessie's pursuits, studies, and amusements.
- Rachel proved an attentive listener, and after Mr. Gresley had furnished her at length with nutritious details respecting **parochial** work, he went on…
- There was no gainsaying this, so Thady started off for Ballycloran, and Father John once more set about performing his **parochial** duties.
- On glancing at the address, the **parochial** functionary observed that it contained no name. The stranger had not gone far, so he made after him to ask it.

pedant ['pədænt]

Definition [*noun*]: A person who pays more attention to formal rules and book learning than they merit
Synonyms: bookworm, scholastic
Examples:

- "We have found another remarkably able leader," said the Prince, "and I have no further anxiety. They all said he was a useless **pedant**, and only I knew better. Reading this letter shows him nothing at all of a **pedant**."
- 'Undoubtedly,' said Rolfe. 'And one is thought a **pedant** and a bore if one ever speaks of it. It's as much against good manners as to begin talking about religion. But a **pedant** must relieve his mind sometimes. I'm so glad I met you today; I wanted to hear what you thought about the boy.'
- No one calls another a Cartesian but he who is one himself, a **pedant** but a **pedant**, a provincial but a provincial; and I would wager it was the printer who put it on the title of Letters to a Provincial.
- Even the best editions of our day have so much of the mere school-book; you feel so often that the man does not regard his author as literature, but simply as text. **Pedant** for **pedant**, the old is better than the new.
- A close observer might have gathered that the topic was distasteful; but the doctor carried it off gaily. "My poor Utterson," said he, "you are unfortunate in such a client. I never saw a man so distressed as you were by my will; unless it were that hide-bound **pedant**, Lanyon, at what he called my scientific heresies. Oh, I know he's a good fellow — you needn't frown—an excellent fellow, and I always mean to see more of him; but a hide-bound **pedant** for all that; an ignorant, blatant **pedant**. I was never more disappointed in any man than Lanyon."

perfidy ['pɜrfɪdi]

Definition [*noun*]: Betrayal of a trust
Synonyms: perfidiousness, treachery
Definition [*noun*]: An act of deliberate betrayal
Synonyms: treachery, betrayal, treason
Examples:
- Heaven be your comforter, my dear friend; summon, I beseech you, your excellent understanding to your aid; let not the **perfidy** of man triumph over the friend of
- "Provided I understand your **perfidy**, sir, and succeed in making you understand that I will be revenged, I shall be reasonable enough," said Albert furiously.

- Outraged pride, the terrors of suspense, the shame and remorse of his own enormous **perfidy** against his only sister, peopled it with spectres.
- "Should any ever determine to rekindle the flames of war, we pray the sovereign reign of all things, who knows the heart, to punish their **perfidy**," etc.
- "Escaped!" exclaimed Herne, springing from his steed, and rushing up to him; "dogs! you have played me false. But your lives shall pay the penalty of your **perfidy**."

ploy [plɔɪ]

Definition [*noun*]: An opening remark intended to secure an advantage for the speaker
Synonyms: gambit
Definition [*noun*]: A maneuver in a game or conversation
Synonyms: gambit, stratagem
Examples:
- "Besides, that kind of **ploy** wouldn't get me much forward. I want to find out what Craw's feared of, for he's damned feared of something. And the key to it is not in Castle Gay."
- "We've been out ever since dinner, sir," said McTurk wearily. One house-match is just like another, and their "**ploy**" of that week happened to be rabbit-shooting with saloon-pistols.
- "He's awfu' restless," she reported. "He's walkin' aboot the floor like a hen on a het girdle. I wish he mayna loss his reason. Dod, I'll warm Erchie's lugs for this **ploy** when I get a haud o' him. [Sic] a job to saddle on a decent wumman!"
- 'Excellent, sir, excellent. When things come to the worst; they will mend; and to the worst they are coming. But as to that nonsense **ploy** of mine, if ye insist on hearing the particulars,' — said the laird, who began to be sensible that the period of telling his story gracefully was gliding fast away.
- Here he stopped, and fixed his eye on the person he addressed with an air of joyful recognition. —'Aye, aye, Mr. Herries of Birrenswork, is this your ainsell in blood and bane? I thought ye had been hanged at Kennington

Common, or Hairiebie, or some of these places, after the
bonny **ploy** ye made in the Forty-five.'

porous ['pourəs]

Definition [*adj*]: Able to absorb fluids
Definition [*adj*]: Full of pores or vessels or holes
Synonyms: poriferous
Antonyms: nonporous
Definition [*adj*]: Allowing passage in and out
Synonyms: holey
Examples:
- "Kízán fukká'a," i.e. thin and slightly **porous**
  earthenware jars used for Fukká'a, a fermented drink,
  made of barley or raisins.
- [* Wherever the rock is visible I perceived compact
  limestone, whitish-grey, partly **porous** and partly with a
  smooth fracture, as in the Jura formation.]
- Tophina; Tuffo, a **porous** stone of volcanic origin, which
  abounds in the neighbourhood of Rome, and, with the
  Travertino, is employed in all common buildings.
- No skylight! no twilight! while Bacchus rules o'er us: No
  thinking! no shrinking! all drinking in chorus: Let us
  moisten our clay, since 'tis thirsty and **porous**: No
  thinking! no shrinking! all drinking in chorus!
- As he felt in July after the fire in John's lodgings, so he
  felt now; just the same again, all over again, only worse.
  The **porous** sandstone was wearing down.

precursor [prɪˈkɜrsər]

Definition [*noun*]: A substance from which another substance is
formed (especially by a metabolic reaction)
Definition [*noun*]: A person who goes before or announces the
coming of another
Synonyms: forerunner
Definition [*noun*]: Something that precedes and indicates the
approach of something or someone
Synonyms: harbinger, forerunner, predecessor, herald
Examples:

- 'I suppose,' said my host, 'that the repeal of the Test Acts will be merely a **precursor** of the emancipation of the Papists?'
- She made an effort to alter her position, but failed: her face changed; she seemed to experience some inward sensation — the **precursor**, perhaps, of the last pang.
- He was the first of our party we had lost, and his death, the sad **precursor** of so many more, cast an additional gloom over us.
- So through the long generations, this heavy **precursor**, this ancestor of all of us, fought and bred and perished, changing almost imperceptibly.
- "It is nothing to do with sides," said Mr. St. Barbe; "this affair goes far beyond sides. The '**Precursor**' wants to put down the Crown; I shall put down the 'Precursor.' It is an affair of the closet, not of sides — an affair of the royal closet, sir. I am acting for the Crown, sir; the Crown has appealed to me. I save the Crown, and there must be personal relations with the highest," and he looked quite fierce.

pristine ['prɪstin]

Definition [*adj*]: Completely free from dirt or contamination
Definition [*adj*]: Immaculately clean and unused
Examples:
- A flash of joy such as he had not perceived on her countenance for weeks transformed its marble-like severity into something of its **pristine** beauty.
- Carrie swallowed this story in all its **pristine** beauty. She sincerely wished he could get through the summer. He looked so hopeless.
- Here Jael, who had been busy pulling back the table, replacing the long row of chairs, and resanding the broad centre Sahara of the room to its dreary, **pristine** aridness, stopped, fairly aghast with amazement.
- Below him, the eternal tremble of pale-earth, unreal waters, far beyond which rose the stiff resistance of mountains losing their **pristine** blue. Distinct, frail distances far off on the dry air, dim-seeing, yet sharp and edged with menace.

- Nobody touched her. Perhaps some had heard of her; a few might even have seen her — driving through Norton Bury in her **pristine** state, as the young 'squire's handsome wife — the charming Lady Caroline.

profound [prə'faʊnd]

Definition [*adj*]: Showing intellectual penetration or emotional depth
Antonyms: superficial
Definition [*adj*]: Of the greatest intensity; complete
Definition [*adj*]: Far-reaching and thoroughgoing in effect especially on the nature of something
Synonyms: fundamental
Definition [*adj*]: Coming from deep within one
Definition [*adj*]: (of sleep) deep and complete
Synonyms: heavy, sound, wakeless
Definition [*adj*]: Situated at or extending to great depth; too deep to have been sounded or plumbed
Synonyms: unfathomed, unplumbed, unsounded
Examples:
- This might be **profound** insight, and it might be profound fatuity. Rowland turned away; he could not trust himself to speak.
- "**Profound**! Profound!" cried Challenger. "Now, my young friend, is it possible that wisdom may come from you where your seniors have so signally failed?"
- "About everything, my dear boy, after the style of Buckle, you know . . . but more **profound**, more profound. . . . Everything will be solved and made clear in it?"
- There are in this world two beings who give a **profound** start — the mother who recovers her child and the tiger who recovers his prey. Javert gave that profound start.
- "Sir," replied Michel, "pleasantry apart, I have a **profound** respect for men of science who do possess science, but a profound contempt for men of science who do not."

reiterate [rɪ'ɪtə,reɪt]

Definition [*verb*]: To say, state, or perform again
Synonyms: repeat, ingeminate, iterate, restate, retell
Examples:

- "Very startling," I answered. "But I must **reiterate** my former remark, that I do not understand in the very least degree what it has to do with us."
- "And I have no doubt," said Mr. Lorry, "that I was right in the conversation we had. My opinion is confirmed, and I **reiterate** my advice."
- "Him! Your duty is not to offend him. Address your excuses to him. I refuse to be dragged over the same ground, to **reiterate** the same command perpetually."
- The lean man with the strident voice ceased firing to turn and **reiterate** his point. "They can't possibly cross," he bawled. "They —"
- "You shall know what it means, Lady Janet, in half an hour. I don't insist — I only **reiterate** my entreaty. Let the man be sent away."

reparation [ˌrɛpəˈreɪʃən]

Definition [*noun*]: Compensation (given or received) for an insult or injury
Definition [*noun*]: (usually plural) compensation exacted from a defeated nation by the victors
Definition [*noun*]: The act of putting something in working order again
Synonyms: repair, fix, fixing, fixture, mend, mending
Definition [*noun*]: Something done or paid in expiation of a wrong
Synonyms: amends
Examples:

- '**Reparation**!' said she. 'Yes, truly! It is easy for him to talk of **reparation**, fresh from journeying and junketing in foreign lands, and living a life of vanity and pleasure. But let him look at me, in prison, and in bonds here. I endure without murmuring, because it is appointed that I shall so make **reparation** for my sins. Reparation! Is there none in this room? Has there been none here this fifteen years?'
- "**Reparation**? To you! It is you who can offer me no **reparation** for the offence against my feelings — and my person; for what reparation can be adequate for your

odious and ridiculous plot so scornful in its implication, so humiliating to my pride. No! I don't want to remember you."
- "**Reparation**, madam!" cried Nowell. "Give back the land you have stolen from me—restore the boundary lines—sign the deed in Sir Ralph's possession—that is the only **reparation** you can make."
- What was my surprise, then, when the will having been proved, I obtained permission to read it and found that it not only contained mention of **reparation**, but that this **reparation** was to be made to Margaret his wife.
- "All the **reparation** in your power to make — all the **reparation** that the whole world can invent could not undo my sin. It and the effects must lie upon me forever."

repugnance [rɪˈpəgnəns]

Definition [*noun*]: Intense aversion
Synonyms: repulsion, revulsion, horror
Definition [*noun*]: The relation between propositions that cannot both be true at the same time
Synonyms: incompatibility, mutual exclusiveness, inconsistency
Examples:
- "I understand your **repugnance**, my child," he said, gently; "your reputation has suffered greatly through the attentions of the marquis."
- "And you may possibly remember," said the king, very deliberately, "that you had the greatest **repugnance** for this marriage."
- Such was his disquietude that he resolved to apply to Chupin, even though this traitor inspired him with extreme **repugnance**.
- First of all, I experienced an invincible **repugnance** on arriving; but oddly enough the life seemed to me less painful than I had imagined on the journey.
- Felton made no reply, took the book with the same appearance of **repugnance** which he had before manifested, and retired pensively.

resonant [ˈrɛzə,nənt]

Definition [adj]: Characterized by resonance
Synonyms: resonating, resounding, reverberating, reverberative
Definition [adj]: Serving to bring to mind
Synonyms: evocative, redolent, remindful, reminiscent
Examples:

- To the page's astonishment, the giant gentleman with the **resonant** bass voice answered this quite gravely. "I'm Benjulia," he said.
- The double reverberation of retreating feet on the heavenborn earth, the double vibration of a Jew's harp in the **resonant** lane.
- His touch on the koto was soft and delicate, and Yūgiri's flute, in the banjiki mode, was wonderfully **resonant**. Kashiwagi could not be persuaded to sing for them.
- 'There's no treachery in my thoughts, and never has been,' said Masha in her distinct, **resonant** voice; 'I've told you already, my heart was heavy.'
- Frozen and mute I heard, . . . the dead silence, and his **resonant** voice vibrating through it, seemed more terrific than the wildest storm.

saturate ['sætʃə,reɪt]

Definition [verb]: Cause (a chemical compound, vapour, solution, magnetic material) to unite with the greatest possible amount of another substance
Definition [verb]: Infuse or fill completely
Synonyms: impregnate
Examples:

- The thing that weighed heaviest on Raggles's soul and clogged his poet's fancy was the spirit of absolute egotism that seemed to saturate the people as toys are **saturated** with paint. Each one that he considered appeared a monster of abominable and insolent conceit. Humanity was gone from them; they were toddling idols of stone and varnish, worshipping themselves and greedy for though oblivious of worship from their fellow graven images. Frozen, cruel, implacable, impervious, cut to an identical pattern, they hurried on their ways like statues brought by some miracles to motion, while soul and feeling lay unaroused in the reluctant marble.

- Larose was **saturating** himself in the atmosphere of 'a suspect,' and, with every sense upon the alert, was endeavouring to grip something of the psychology of the man who was standing by his side.
- "Only I was afraid you would be getting so learned," said Celia, regarding Mr. Casaubon's learning as a kind of damp which might in due time **saturate** a neighboring body.
- Yet he wanted something. He was happy in the wet hillside, that was overgrown and obscure with bushes and flowers. He wanted to touch them all, to **saturate** himself with the touch of them all. He took off his clothes, and sat down naked among the primroses, moving his feet softly among the primroses, his legs, his knees, his arms right up to the arm-pits, lying down and letting them touch his belly, his breasts. It was such a fine, cool, subtle touch all over him, he seemed to saturate himself with their contact.

seethe [*sið*]

Definition [*verb*]: Be noisy with activity
Synonyms: hum, buzz
Definition [*verb*]: Be in an agitated emotional state
Synonyms: boil
Definition [*verb*]: Foam as if boiling
Definition [*verb*]: Boil vigorously
Synonyms: roll
Examples:
- All this stir and seethe of lights and people was but the rim, the shores of a great inner darkness and void. She wanted very much to be on the **seething**, partially illuminated shore, for within her was the void reality of dark space.
- His heart went back to the savage old spirit of the place: the desire for old gods, old, lost passions, the passion of the cold-blooded, darting snakes that hissed and shot away from him, the mystery of blood-sacrifices, all the lost, intense sensations of the primeval people of the place, whose passions **seethed** in the air still, from those long days before the Romans came. The seethe of

a lost, dark passion in the air. The presence of unseen snakes.

- The **seething** cauldron of lower life, **seething** on the very tissue of the higher life, **seething** the soul away, seething at the marrow. The vast and unrelenting will of the swarming lower life, working forever against man's attempt at a higher life, a further created being.
- And he said unto them, this is that which the LORD hath said, Tomorrow is the rest of the holy Sabbath unto the LORD: bake that which ye will bake to day, and **seethe** that ye will seethe; and that which remaineth over lay up for you to be kept until the morning.
- Take the choice of the flock, and burn also the bones under it, and make it boil well, and let them **seethe** the bones of it therein.

sensory ['sɛnsəri]

Definition [*adj*]: Of a nerve fiber or impulse originating outside and passing toward the central nervous system
Synonyms: centripetal, receptive
Definition [*adj*]: Involving or derived from the senses
Synonyms: sensorial
Antonyms: extrasensory
Definition [*adj*]: Relating to or concerned in sensation
Synonyms: sensational
Examples:

- The stimulus excites the peripheral sense-organ adequately for a current to pass into the **sensory** nerve; 2. The sensory nerve is traversed; 3. The transformation (or reflection) of the sensory into a motor current occurs in the centres; 4. The spinal cord and motor nerve are traversed; 5. The motor current excites the muscle to the contracting point.
- Whenever the sources of dreams are completely enumerated they fall into the following four categories, which have also been employed in the classification of dreams: (1) external (objective) **sensory** stimuli; (2) internal (subjective) **sensory** stimuli; (3) internal (organic) physical stimuli; (4) Purely psychical sources of excitation.

- Probability — It is fairly clear that scientific laws are compendious descriptions of past **sensory** experience, or at the very least formulae from which such descriptions can be derived; but by what right do we use them also for prediction of future sensory experiences?
- The younger Strumpell, the son of the philosopher, whose work on dreams has already more than once served us as a guide in considering the problems of dreams, has, as is well known, recorded his observations of a patient afflicted with general anaesthesia of the skin and with paralysis of several of the higher **sensory** organs. This man would laps into sleep whenever the few remaining **sensory** paths between himself and the outer world were closed. When we wish to fall asleep we are accustomed to strive for a condition similar to that obtaining in Strumpell's experiment. We close the most important sensory portals, the eyes, and we endeavour to protect the other senses from all stimuli or from any change of the stimuli already acting upon them. We then fall asleep, although our preparations are never wholly successful. For we can never completely insulate the **sensory** organs, nor can we entirely abolish the excitability of the **sensory** organs themselves. That we may at any time be awakened by intenser stimuli should prove to us "that the mind has remained in constant communication with the external world even during sleep." The **sensory** stimuli that reach us during sleep may easily become the source of dreams.
- A man's body, as we perceive it, is a system of **sensory** characters, such as colour, shape, softness. This system, in spite of large fluctuations due to the voluntary movement of limbs, remains on the whole constant in form, and lies permanently at the centre of his perceived world. In fact, his body is made up of visual appearances, tactual "appearances" (as when he strokes or pushes his head with his hand), sensations of warmth, cold, pressure, pain, on the surface of his perceived body's shape or within its interior. The changeful three-dimensional shape of his body is really an abstraction, a formula derived from the spatial relations of this host of **sensory** characters, which constitute his body, and the relations of this **sensory**

system to the other host of sensory characters, which constitute external physical objects.

somber ['sɑmbər]

Definition [*adj*]: Lacking brightness or color; dull
Synonyms: drab, sober, sombre
Definition [*adj*]: Grave or even gloomy in character
Synonyms: sombre, melancholy
Examples:

- The country, **somber** in the somber night. The vast open country. What monotonous desolation! Rapidly, through the vast silent spaces, the little car glided over the lonely route into the black arms of the pines.
- "Is that true?" demanded Feodor Feodorovitch, with his most **somber** manner. "Is it true, Koupriane, that you have nothing?"
- The eyes of the Puritan flashed, but only once, and his countenance, for an instant, illuminated by that flash, resumed its **somber** impassibility.
- Rybin rose to his feet **somber** and powerful. His face darkened, his beard quivered as if he ground his teeth inaudibly, and he continued in a lowered voice:
- In an instant the **somber** sky was confounded with the sea of snow which the wind raised up from the earth. Everything was indistinguishable.

sporadic [spoʊ'rædɪk]

Definition [*adj*]: Recurring in scattered and irregular or unpredictable instances
Antonyms: continual
Examples:

- Chap. VI. describes one of the **sporadic** outcrops near Tayyib Ism; and Chap. IX notices the apparently volcanic sulphur-mount near El–Muwaylah.
- 'Don't know,' said the Deputy Commissioner reflectively. 'We've got locusts with us. There's **sporadic** cholera all along the north — at least we're calling it **sporadic** for decency's sake. The spring crops are short in five districts, and nobody seems to know where the rains

are. It's nearly March now. I don't want to scare anybody, but it seems to me that Nature's going to audit her accounts with a big red pencil this summer.'
- "Even if it was plague, which is not certain," said Inchcape Jones, "there's no reason to cause a row and frighten everybody. It was a **sporadic** case. There won't be any more."
- Of larks there are two kinds. One lives on the ground and has a crest on its head; the other is gregarious, and not **sporadic** like the first; it is, however, of the same coloured plumage, but is smaller, and has no crest; it is an article of human food.
- But every imitative phenomenon must once have had its original, and I propose that for the future we keep as close as may be to the more first-hand and original forms of experience. These are more likely to be found in **sporadic** adult cases.

staid [*steɪd*]

Definition [*adj*]: Characterized by dignity and propriety
Synonyms: sedate
Examples:
- "Indeed, Lady Bellaston," said he, "I don't wonder you are astonished at the length of my visit; for I have **staid** above two hours, and I did not think I had **staid** above half-a-one."
- 'No no, I would rather that it **staid** — cruel as it is, I would rather that it **staid**,' rejoined the child. 'I am not afraid to have it in my sleep, but I am so sad — so very, very sad.'
- I desired several times, while he **staid**, to have leave to retire to my apartment; but was denied. The search, I suppose, was not over.
- Five of the soldiers, who did not go into the tent, but **staid** under the tree during the rain, complained much of headache and uneasiness at stomach.
- Abbey Street was a quiet, **staid** place behind Tullie House. It was a thin house with neat stone steps and a light in the upper window.

substantiate [səb'stænʃi,eɪt]

Definition [*verb*]: Establish or strengthen as with new evidence or facts
Synonyms: confirm, corroborate, sustain, support, affirm
Antonyms: negate
Definition [*verb*]: Represent in bodily form
Synonyms: incarnate, body forth, embody
Definition [*verb*]: Make real or concrete; give reality or substance to
Synonyms: realize, realise, actualize, actualise
Definition [*verb*]: Solidify, firm, or strengthen
Examples:

- 'Let them find themselves again, and their own universe, and their own gods. Let them **substantiate** their own mysteries. The Irish have been so wordy about their far-off heroes and green days of the heroic gods. Now tell them to substantiate them, as we have tried to substantiate Quetzalcoatl and Huitzilopochtli.'
- "And these are the papers **substantiating** your statements?" asked Peter Drew, handing up a small parcel of faded newspapers for him to examine.
- All possibilities were over; the meeting was stultified. Yet it was almost visible to her in her fantasy even now, though it could never be substantiated...
- "Alas! Alas!" she cried, in accents of despair. "But who will claim it?—and how can the claim be substantiated?" she added, recovering herself in some degree.
- He then fully **substantiated** all the statements of the other, adding other facts of the same character, known only to himself.

succumb [sə'kəm]

Definition [*verb*]: Consent reluctantly
Synonyms: yield, give in, knuckle under, buckle under
Definition [*verb*]: Be fatally overwhelmed
Synonyms: yield
Antonyms: survive
Examples:

- "It's a catching complaint, you see, Mr. Levy," said Raffles, "especially when one's elders and betters themselves **succumb** to it."
- Then was there again spoken unto me without voice: "What matter about thyself, Zarathustra! Speak thy word, and **succumb**!"
- "I can give a reason,—a good reason,—a reason which I cannot oppose, though it must be fatal to me unless I can remove it; a reason to which I must **succumb** if necessary, but to which, Marion, I will not succumb at once. If you say that you cannot love me that will be a reason."
- She was an old, wrinkled and austere rustic, who seemed always to **succumb** to the pressure of new customs with a kind of contempt.
- Nay! Nay! Three times Nay! Always more, always better ones of your type shall succumb—for ye shall always have it worse and harder. Thus only…

supersede [ˌsupər'sid]

Definition [*verb*]: Take the place or move into the position of
Synonyms: supplant, replace, supervene upon
Examples:
- As the necessity of sleep seems rather to depend upon the body than the mind, it does not appear how the improvement of the mind can tend very greatly to supersede this 'conspicuous infirmity'. A man who by great excitements on his mind is able to pass two or three nights without sleep, proportionably exhausts the vigour of his body, and this diminution of health and strength will soon disturb the operations of his understanding, so that by these great efforts he appears to have made no real progress whatever in **superseding** the necessity of this species of rest.
- "Be explicit . . . Speak for themselves . . . make you see that their painters are already **superseding** some of the better known . . . "
- The lyric movement of the Chorus from Hellas, which I propose to quote, marks the highest point of Shelley's rhythmical invention. As for the matter expressed in it, we must not forget that these stanzas are written for a

Chorus of Greek captive women, whose creed does not prevent their feeling a regret for the "mightier forms of an older, austerer worship." Shelley's note reminds the reader, with characteristic caution and frankness, that "the popular notions of Christianity are represented in this Chorus as true in their relation to the worship they **superseded**, and that which in all probability they will supersede, without considering their merits in a relation more universal."

- This officer shall **supersede** even the Sheriff in possession, excepting by an extent for the king; only with this provision…
- "You need not act upon the will," said Jan. "There was a codicil, you know, **superseding** it, though it can't be found. Sibylla's your cousin—it would be a cruel thing to turn her from her home."

talon ['tælən]

Definition [*noun*]: A sharp hooked claw especially on a bird of prey

Examples:
- These are only the vultures and jackal prowlers in Love's wake, ready to pounce on the faint hearted pilgrim who through weakness falls into the rear, where fang and **talon** lie in wait to swoop down and rend him.
- "Why? We are only strong as tigers are strong — just the strength of the **talon** and fang. I do not know. I was weak as water once; I may be again, if — if ——"
- And she is angry. There is something stupid, absurd, in the hard, **talon**-like eyes watching so fiercely and so confidently in the doorway, sure, unmitigated. Has the creature no sense?
- The hand of the shadow emerged from beneath its mantle and descended upon the arm of Phoebus with the grip of an eagle's **talon**; at the same time the shadow spoke…
- So the case stood with respect to our pretty hostess; but, before proceeding further, it may be well to give a more complete description of the two birds of prey by whom she was threatened with beak and **talon**.

tangential [tænˈdʒɛnʃəl]

Definition [*adj*]: Of superficial relevance if any
Synonyms: digressive
Definition [*adj*]: Of or relating to or acting along or in the direction of a tangent
Examples:

- Adela shook her head. "I suppose I imagine rather intensely," she said. "I seem to see things obliquely, if you know what I mean. They're alongside the actual thing, a sort of tangent. I think really that's what all art is- **tangential**." The word had hardly left her lips when a voice, tangential to her ear, said: "Do let me persuade you, Miss Hunt."

- If two circles one lying within the other are in contact, and if any straight line be drawn tangent to the inner circle, cutting the outer circle, and if three lines be drawn from the point at which the circles are in contact to three points on the **tangential** straight line, namely, the point of tangency on the inner circle and the two points where the straight line extended cuts the outer circle, then these three lines will contain equal angles at the point of contact.

- Of a truth the first and foremost step in all knowledge of mankind is the conviction that a man's conduct, taken as a whole, and in all its essential particulars, is not governed by his reason or by any of the resolutions which he may make in virtue of it. No man becomes this or that by wishing to be it, however earnestly. His acts proceed from his innate and unalterable character, and they are more immediately and particularly determined by motives. A man's conduct, therefore, is the necessary product of both character and motive. It may be illustrated by the course of a planet, which is the result of the combined effect of the **tangential** energy with which it is endowed, and the centripetal energy which operates from the sun. In this simile the former energy represents character, and the latter the influence of motive. It is almost more than a mere simile. The tangential energy which properly speaking is the source of the planet's motion, whilst on the other hand the motion is kept in check by gravitation, is, from a metaphysical point of view, the will manifesting itself in that body.

- He spread his mental and spiritual equipment before them very artlessly. Their isolation and their immense concentration on each other had made them sensitive to personal quality, and they listened to the broken English and the queer **tangential** starts into new topics of this dirty mongrel creature with the keenest appreciation of its quality. It was inconsistent, miscellaneous, simple, honest, and human. It was as touching as the medley in the pocket of a dead schoolboy. He was superstitious and skeptical and sensual and spiritual, and very, very earnest. The things he believed, even if they were just beliefs about the weather or drying venison or filling pipes, he believed with emotion. He flushed as he told them. For all his intellectual muddle they felt he knew how to live honestly and die if need be very finely.

tangible [ˈtændʒəbəl]

Definition [*adj*]: Perceptible by the senses especially the sense of touch
Synonyms: touchable
Antonyms: intangible
Definition [*adj*]: Capable of being treated as fact
Synonyms: real
Definition [*adj*]: (of especially business assets) having physical substance and intrinsic monetary value
Antonyms: intangible
Definition [*adj*]: Capable of being perceived; especially capable of being handled or touched or felt
Synonyms: palpable
Antonyms: impalpable
Examples:
- That all fluid bodies which we may call **tangible**, are nothing but some more subtle parts of those particles, that serve to constitute all tangible bodies.
- Thus let the nature in question be the action and motion of the spirit enclosed in **tangible** bodies. For everything **tangible** that we are acquainted with contains an invisible and intangible spirit which it wraps and clothes as with a garment. Hence that three-fold source, so potent and wonderful, of the process of the spirit in a **tangible** body. For the spirit in a **tangible** substance, if

discharged, contracts bodies and dries them up; if detained, softens and melts them; if neither wholly discharged nor wholly detained, gives them shape, produces limbs, assimilates, digests, ejects, organizes, and the like. And all these processes are made manifest to the sense by conspicuous effects.

- We may illustrate this by considering the sense of feeling, and the imaginary distance or interval interposed betwixt **tangible** or solid objects. I suppose two cases, viz. that of a man supported in the air, and moving his limbs to and fro, without meeting anything tangible; and that of a man, who feeling something tangible, leaves it, and after a motion, of which he is sensible, perceives another tangible object; and I then ask, wherein consists the difference betwixt these two cases? No one will make any scruple to affirm, that it consists merely in the perceiving those objects, and that the sensation, which arises from the motion, is in both cases the same: And as that sensation is not capable of conveying to us an idea of extension, when unaccompanied with some other perception, it can no more give us that idea, when mixed with the impressions of **tangible** objects; since that mixture produces no alteration upon it.

- I answer, it must be acknowledged, the visible Square is fitter than the visible Circle, to represent the **tangible** Square, but then it is not because it is liker, or more of a Species with it; but because the visible Square contains in it several distinct Parts, whereby to mark the several distinct, corresponding Parts of a tangible Square, whereas the visible Circle doth not. The Square perceived by Touch, hath four distinct, equal Sides, so also hath it four distinct, equal Angles. It is therefore necessary, that the visible Figure which shall be most proper to mark it, contain four distinct equal Parts corresponding to the four Sides of the **tangible** Square; as likewise four other distinct and equal Parts, whereby to denote the four equal Angles of the tangible Square. And accordingly we see the visible Figures contain in them distinct visible Parts, answering to the distinct tangible Parts of the Figures signified, or suggested by them.

- But though motion and darkness, either alone, or attended with **tangible** and visible objects, convey no idea of a vacuum or extension without matter, yet they are the causes why we falsely imagine we can form such an idea. For there is a close relation betwixt that motion and darkness, and a real extension, or composition of visible and tangible objects.

tarnish ['tarnɪʃ]

Definition [*noun*]: Discoloration of metal surface caused by oxidation
Definition [*verb*]: Make dirty or spotty, as by exposure to air; also used metaphorically
Synonyms: stain, maculate, sully, defile
Examples:
- Now, that the Fly is able to walk on Glass, proceeds partly from some ruggedness of the surface: and chiefly from a kind of **tarnish**, or dirty smoaky substance, which adheres to the surface of that very hard body; and though the pointed parts cannot penetrate the substance of Glass, yet may they find pores enough in the **tarnish**, or at least make them.
- "Why didn't she sell some of that silver? All those platters and covered dishes stuck away with the **tarnish** of years on them!"
- "Golden hair (experto crede) does not **tarnish** in the tomb. Read the last paragraph in Zola's Nana which physiologically is astoundingly accurate."
- White hands cling to the tightened rein, Slipping the spur from the booted heel, tenderest voices cry, 'Turn again,' Red lips **tarnish** the scabbarded steel, High hopes faint on a warm hearth-stone — He travels the fastest who travels alone.
- Well, it was glorious news for her. But, as if to **tarnish** its delight, like an envious sprite of evil, deep down in her mind lay that other news, just read—the ambiguous remark of old Mrs. Peveril's.

tawdry ['tɔdri]

Definition [*adj*]: Tastelessly showy

Synonyms: brassy, cheap, flash, flashy, garish, gaudy, gimcrack, loud, meretricious, tacky, tatty, trashy
Definition [*adj*]: Cheap and shoddy
Synonyms: cheapjack, shoddy
Examples:

- "**Tawdry**! Pitiful! Carol — the clean girl that used to walk so fast! — sneaking and tittering in dark corners, being sentimental and jealous at church suppers!"
- He turned round. A buxom woman in a **tawdry** and tattered gown was running towards him as fast as her natural impediments to quick progression would permit.
- "Ah, yes!" cried the girl, clasping her dark hands, which gleamed with **tawdry** rings; "and his daughter, too, how I love her!"
- 'Do you admire my fountain and my birds?' she continued, after a short pause. 'After Armine, Ducie appears a little **tawdry** toy.'
- She pitied herself that her romance should be pitiful; she sighed that in this colorless hour, to this austere self, it should seem **tawdry**.

thwart [*thwɔrt*]

Definition [*noun*]: A crosspiece spreading the gunnels of a boat; used as a seat in a rowboat
Synonyms: cross thwart
Definition [*verb*]: Hinder or prevent (the efforts, plans, or desires) of
Synonyms: queer, spoil, scotch, foil, cross, frustrate, baffle, bilk
Examples:

- "**Thwart** him?" quoth her wazeer, gaping at the swift energy of mind and body with which this woman was endowed, the like of which he had never seen in any woman yet. "Thwart him?" he repeated.
- "My lady — my good, kind mistress!" she cried, vehemently, "don't try to **thwart** me in this — don't ask me to **thwart** him. I tell you I must marry him. You don't know what he is. It will be my ruin, and the ruin of others, if I break my word. I must marry him!"
- "Treat you with contempt? Don't let you have any will of your own? **Thwart** you in all ways?" he repeated. "Who says it, Selina?"

- The next day we came **thwart** of Gabriel's Island, and at eight of the clock at night we had the Cape Labrador west from us ten leagues.

tractable ['træktəbəl]

Definition [*adj*]: Easily managed (controlled or taught or molded)
Synonyms: manipulable
Antonyms: intractable
Definition [*adj*]: Readily reacting to suggestions and influences
Synonyms: amenable
Examples:
- 'The point I wish to establish is, that Miss Helstone, though gentle, **tractable**, and candid enough, is still perfectly capable of defying even Mr. Moore's penetration.'
- "Besides, Jane's children are infinitely more **tractable** than poor Emma's," was John's parting shot. Strange, thought Mary, how attached John was to his second family.
- "Her mother had made her swear that she would not be **tractable**, and you need not hope to possess her without the mother's consent."
- Still deeply seized by some inward grief, but **tractable**, he allowed Quigg to lead him away and down the street to a little park.
- This last consideration rendered Foster **tractable**; he only asked permission to ride before, to make matters ready, and spurring his horse, he posted before the litter, while Varney falling about threescore paces behind it, it remained only attended by Tider.

unadulterated [ˌʌnʌ'dʌltɜr,eɪtɪd]

Definition [*adj*]: Not mixed with impurities
Definition [*adj*]: Without qualification; used informally as (often pejorative) intensifiers
Synonyms: arrant, complete, consummate, double-dyed, everlasting, gross, perfect, pure, sodding, stark, staring, thoroughgoing, utter
Examples:

- 'I look upon an Orangeman,' said Coningsby, 'as a pure Whig; the only professor and practiser of **unadulterated** Whiggism.'
- Mr. Halder, the leader of this triumvirate, was the particular patron of Girt, the young perfumer; and, though his superior in birth and riches, was scarcely upon a par with him, from willful neglect, in education; and undoubtedly beneath him in decency and conduct, notwithstanding young Girt piqued himself far less upon such sentimental qualifications, than upon his skill in cosmetics, and had less respect for **unadulterated** morals, than **unadulterated** powder.
- SOCRATES: How can there be purity in whiteness, and what purity? Is that purest which is greatest or most in quantity, or that which is most **unadulterated** and freest from any admixture of other colours?
- "Ah, that is human nature, Sergeant! pure, **unadulterated** Scotch human nature. A cake, man, to say the truth, is an agreeable morsel, and I often see the time when I pine for a bite myself."
- His face was also like margarine, but of **adulterated** margarine, certainly. By the side of it, his cranium, the color of **unadulterated** margarine, looked almost like butter, by comparison.

usury [ˈjuʒəri]

Definition [*noun*]: An exorbitant or unlawful rate of interest
Synonyms: vigorish
Definition [*noun*]: The act of lending money at an exorbitant rate of interest
Examples:
- Thou shalt not lend upon **usury** to thy brother; usury of money, usury of victuals, usury of anything that is lent upon usury.
- Those who devour **usury** shall not rise again, save as he riseth whom Satan hath paralysed with a touch; and that is because they say 'selling is only like **usury**,' but God has made selling lawful and **usury** unlawful; and he to whom the admonition from his Lord has come, if he desists, what has gone before is his: his matter is in God's hands. But whosoever returns (to usury) these are

the fellows of the Fire, and they shall dwell therein for aye. God shall blot out **usury**, but shall make almsgiving profit-able, for God loves not any sinful misbeliever.

- If it be objected that this doth in a sort authorize **usury**, which before, was in some places but permissive; the answer is, that it is better to mitigate **usury**, by declaration, than to suffer it to rage, by connivance.

- To speak now of the reformation, and reiglement, of **usury**; how the discommodities of it may be best avoided, and the commodities retained. It appears, by the balance of commodities and discommodities of **usury**, two things are to be reconciled. The one, that the tooth of usury be grinded, that it bite not too much; the other, that there be left open a means, to invite moneyed men to lend to the merchants, for the continuing and quickening of trade. This cannot be done, except you introduce two several sorts of usury, a less and a greater. For if you reduce usury to one low rate, it will ease the common borrower, but the merchant will be to seek for money. And it is to be noted, that the trade of merchandize, being the most lucrative, may bear **usury** at a good rate; other contracts not so.

- I told him my desires humbly, in quavering syllables. In return, he craved my antecedents and residence, pried into my private life, insolently demanded how many children had I and did I live in wedlock, and asked divers other unseemly and degrading questions. Ay, I was treated like a thief convicted before the act, till I produced my certificates of goods and chattels aforementioned. Never had they appeared so insignificant and paltry as then, when he sniffed over them with the air of one disdainfully doing a disagreeable task. It is said, "Thou shalt not lend upon **usury** to thy brother; usury of money, usury of victuals, **usury** of anything that is lent upon **usury**"; but he evidently was not my brother, for he demanded seventy per cent. I put my signature to certain indentures, received my pottage, and fled from his presence.

verbose [vər'boʊs]

Definition [*adj*]: Using or containing too many words

Synonyms: long-winded, tedious, windy, wordy
Examples:
- "Very pretty," sneered Mr. Ram, "and most eloquent too. But then Henry Muffins always was **verbose** and windy, always a man of froth."
- "Read us poetry!" I cannot describe the desolation which fell upon us as she opened a little volume and mouthed out the **verbose**, sentimental foolery which it contained.
- "A pure Christianity, unstained by blood and perjury, by hypocrisy and **verbose** genuflection. Can I not worship and say my prayers among the clouds?" And she pointed to the lofty ceiling and the handsome chandelier.
- "Well, go on," said the man who had just admitted he took chloral, testily, "and get it over, quick. You are not addressing the Cosmopolitan Investment Company now. You have been too **verbose** all along."
- 'Good ——Then, to make the matter clear to you I must begin by telling you a story, if I may trespass on your patience to that extent. I will endeavour not to be more **verbose** than the occasion requires.'

verdict [ˈvɜrdɪkt]

Definition [*noun*]: (law) the findings of a jury on issues of fact submitted to it for decision; can be used in formulating a judgment
Synonyms: finding of fact
Examples:
- If the judge has adjourned the court to his own lodgings, and there receives the **verdict**, it is a public and not a privy **verdict**.
- The man was a rogue, however we take him, and the sole tangible fact is that a report of the evidence given at the inquest did exist, and that the **verdict** may have been 'Accidental Death.' We do not know but that an open verdict was given. Appleyard professes to have been convinced by the evidence, not by the **verdict**.
- "If you think that, then it is your imperative duty to acquit the prisoner at the bar. The only **verdict** which you dare give is a verdict of 'Not Guilty'."
- Lady Mary covered her face with her hands. She seemed to read in Ruff's words the **verdict** of the two

men—the **verdict** of common sense. Nevertheless, he
made one more request before leaving.

- A VERDICT, vere dictum, is either privy, or public. A
privy **verdict** is when the judge has left or adjourned the
court; and the jury, being agreed, in order to be delivered
from their confinement, obtain leave to give their verdict
privily to the judge out of court: which privy verdict is of
no force, unless afterwards affirmed by a public verdict
given openly in court; wherein the jury may, if they
please, vary from their privy **verdict**. So that the privy
verdict is indeed a mere nullity; and yet it is a
dangerous practice, allowing time for the parties to
tamper with the jury, and therefore very seldom
indulged. But the only effectual and legal verdict is the
public verdict; in which they openly declare to have
found the issue for the plaintiff, or for the defendant; and
if for the plaintiff, they assess the damages also
sustained by the plaintiff, in consequence of the injury
upon which the action is brought.

viable [ˈvaɪəbəl]

Definition [*adj*]: Capable of being done with means at hand and
circumstances as they are
Synonyms: feasible, executable, practicable, workable
Definition [*adj*]: Capable of life or normal growth and
development
Examples:

- 'It seems that he had climbed for a few days with one of
the Kronigs and Dupont, and they had done some hair-
raising things on the Aiguilles. Dupont told me that they
had found a new route up the Montanvert side of the
Charmoz. He said that Hollond climbed like a **Viable**
fou,' and if you know Dupont's standard of madness you
will see that the pace must have been pretty hot. "But
Monsieur was sick," he added; "his eyes were not good.
And I and Franz, we were grieved for him and a little
afraid. We were glad when he left us."
- Just been — not grinding, alas! — I couldn't — but doing
a bit of Fontainebleau. I don't think I'll be plucked. I am
not sure though — I am so busy, what with this d-d law,
and this Fontainebleau always at my elbow, and three

plays (three, think of that!) and a story, all crying out to me, 'Finish, finish, make an entire end, make us strong, shapely, **viable** creatures!' It's enough to put a man crazy. Moreover, I have my thesis given out now, which is a fifth (is it fifth? I can't count) incumbrance.

- All this manual work was entered into rather as sport than as toil, for it had never been a tyranny. The most serious attention of every member was given to very different matters. The younger islanders spent much time in the library and the lab, absorbing the culture of the inferior species. The elders were concerned with a prolonged research into the physical and mental attributes of their own kind. In particular they were grappling with the problem of breeding. At what age might their young women safely conceive? Or should reproduction be ectogenetic? And how could they ensure that the offspring should be both **viable** and supernormal? This research was evidently the chief work of the laboratory. Originally its aim had been mainly practical, but even after the discovery of their impending doom the islanders continued these biological experiments for their theoretical interest.

vituperate [vaɪˈtupəˌreɪt]

Definition [*verb*]: Spread negative information about
Synonyms: vilify, revile, rail
Examples:
- Tell Borya, Mitya, and Andrushka that I **vituperate** them. In the pocket of my greatcoat I found some notes on which was scrawled: "Anton Pavlovitch, for shame, for shame, for shame!" O pessimi discipuli! Utinam vos lupus devoret!
- A quick movement, a slight click, a hustle from the wondering crowd more immediately around, and the handcuffs were on. Utter amazement alone prevented Mr. Drake from knocking down the policeman. A dozen **vituperating** tongues assailed him.
- In the meantime the infant whom he was holding all the time in his arms very tenderly whilst he was

vituperating, shut its eyes languidly; a sign of repletion. Ursus examined the phial, and grumbled…

- "Three months later he strove wildly to free himself from those invincible and invisible bonds with which such a friendship chains our lives. She kept him under her influence, tyrannizing over him, making his life a burden to him. They quarreled continually, **vituperating** and finally fighting each other.

- So he said what soothing things he could, and Esther caught them up, disfigured them, and flung them back at him with scorn. She reproached him with no longer caring for her; she **vituperated** the conduct of his family in never taking the smallest notice of her marriage; and she detailed the insolence of the landlady, who had told her that morning she pitied "poor Mr. Willoughby," and had refused to go out and buy herrings for Esther's early dinner.

vociferous [vou'sɪfərəs]

Definition [*adj*]: Conspicuously and offensively loud; given to vehement outcry
Synonyms: blatant, clamant, clamorous, strident
Examples:

- In about half an hour, the grumbling of the pilot, who was despotic master of the boat, was changed into loud and **vociferous** oaths.

- "Great news! Great news!" cried the urchin, imitating his **vociferous** originals in the street; "all about the famous Captain Lovett, as large as life!"

- And they bowed. And their apparent enthusiasm was all the more **vociferous** on account of the rage and fear that filled their hearts.

- What was he saying? Neither the baron nor the priest could distinguish his words, but when he ceased, the most **vociferous** acclamations rent the air.

- The only audience at the concert was the baby, who however gave such **vociferous** applause that the performers, presuming it to amount to an encore, commenced again.

witting [ˈwɪtɪŋ]

Definition [*adj*]: Aware or knowing
Antonyms: unwitting
Definition [*adj*]: Intentionally conceived
Synonyms: conscious
Examples:

- In feverish doze he thought of bygone days, When love was soft, life strong, and a sweet name, The first sweet name that led him down love's ways, Unbidden ever to his fresh lips came; Half **witting** would he speak it, and for shame Flush red, and think what folk would deem thereof if they might know Œnone was his love.
- The King himself giveth him blows so heavy that the Queen and all they that were at the windows marvelled how Perceval might abide such buffets. The King took **witting** of the shield that Perceval bare, and looketh on it of a long space.
- "Oigh! Oigh!" exclaimed Dougal, softening the sharp exclamations of his surprise as he looked around with an eye of watchful alarm —"Oigh! to see you here — to see you here! — Oigh! — what will come o' ye gin the bailies suld come to get **witting** — ta filthy, gutty hallions, tat they are?"
- Then the lord of the earl-folk to every and each one 1050 of them who with Beowulf the sea-ways had worn then and there on the mead-bench did handsel them treasure, an heir-loom to wit; for him also he bade it That a were-gild be paid, whom Grendel aforetime by wickedness quell'd, as far more of them would he, Save from them God all-**witting** the weird away wended, And that man's mood withal. But the Maker all wielded Of the kindred of mankind, as yet now he doeth. Therefore through-witting will be the best everywhere and the forethought of mind. Many things must abide 1060 Of life and of loth, he who here a long while in these days of the strife with the world shall be dealing.

zeal [zil]

Definition [*noun*]: A feeling of strong eagerness (usually in favor of a person or cause)

Synonyms: ardor, ardour, elan
Definition [*noun*]: Excessive fervor to do something or accomplish some end
Definition [*noun*]: Prompt willingness
Synonyms: readiness, eagerness, forwardness
Examples:

- **Zeal**, light. Four kinds of persons: **zeal** without knowledge; knowledge without **zeal**; neither knowledge nor zeal; both zeal and knowledge. The first three condemned him. The last acquitted him, were excommunicated by the Church and yet saved the Church.
- Through **zeal** knowledge is gotten, through lack of **zeal** knowledge is lost; let a man who knows this double path of gain and loss thus place himself that knowledge may grow.
- And the new **zeal** had ceased to be healthy in its tone as the old **zeal** was: for now the fierce demon Mammon was making his voice heard in this matter.
- 'Not so well as Miss Barfoot, but I think very highly of her. Her **zeal** makes her exaggerate a little now and then, but then the **zeal** is so splendid. I haven't it myself — not in that form.'
- The **zeal** of the Jews for their law and their temple (Josephus, and Philo the Jew, Ad Caium). What other people had such a **zeal**? It was necessary they should have it.

Matching Games

Vocabulary 1

complement • pedant • effigy • disenfranchised • accustomed • gl
ean • culminate • unadulterated • docile •verbose • nebulous •
inadvertent

Pairing Quiz 1

1. accustomed	a. a word or phrase used to complete a grammatical construction
2. effigy	b. a person who pays more attention to formal rules and book learning than they merit
3. verbose	c. a representation of a person (especially in the form of sculpture)
4. disenfranchised	d. deprived of voting rights
5. complement	e. to make psychologically or physically used (to something)
6. docile	f. gather, as of natural products
7. culminate	g. end, especially to reach a final or climactic stage
8. nebulous	h. not mixed with impurities
9. pedant	i. willing to be taught or led or supervised or directed
10. glean	j. using or containing too many words
11. inadvertent	k. lacking definite form or limits
12. unadulterated	l. happening by chance or unexpectedly or unintentionally

Vocabulary 2

cabal • lien • denizen • seethe • forebode • accustomed •
exhilarating • errant • sporadic • auspicious • invidious • pristine

Pairing Quiz 2

1. exhilarating

a. a clique (often secret) that seeks power usually through intrigue

2. seethe

b. the right to take another's property if an obligation is not discharged

3. sporadic

c. a person who inhabits a particular place

4. accustomed

d. to be full of unexpressed anger

5. forebode

e. make a prediction about; tell in advance

6. denizen

f. make psychologically or physically used (to something)

7. auspicious

g. fill with sublime emotion

8. cabal

h. straying from the right course or from accepted standards

9. pristine

i. recurring in scattered and irregular or unpredictable instances

10. invidious

j. auguring favorable circumstances and good luck

11. errant

k. containing or implying a slight or showing prejudice

12. lien

l. completely free from dirt or contamination

Vocabulary 3

ascetic • ploy • burnish • appall • succumb • disobey •
substantiate • tangential • mendacious • dormant • porous •
sensory

Pairing Quiz 3

1. ascetic

a. practicing self-denial as a spiritual discipline

2. mendacious

b. an opening remark intended to secure an advantage for the speaker

3. sensory

c. the property of being smooth and shiny

4. tangential

d. strike with disgust or revulsion

5. substantiate

e. consent reluctantly

6. burnish

f. refuse to go along with; refuse to follow; be disobedient

7. dormant

g. to establish or strengthen as with new evidence or facts

8. ploy

h. of superficial relevance if any

9. disobey

i. given to lying

10. appall

j. in a condition of biological rest or suspended animation

11. succumb

k. able to absorb fluids

12. porous

l. of a nerve fiber or impulse originating outside and passing toward the central nervous system

Vocabulary 4

censor • bombast • nettle • admonish • objurgate • cajole • super
sede • vociferous • artful • profound • staid

Pairing Quiz 4

1. nettle

a. to erase unacceptable parts of something

2. vociferous

b. pompous or pretentious talk or writing

3. bombast

c. to irritate or annoy someone

4. objurgate

d. to counsel in terms of someone's behavior

5. artful

e. express strong disapproval of

6. staid

f. influence or urge by gentle urging, caressing, or flattering

7. admonish

g. take the place or move into the position of

8. supersede

h. conspicuously and offensively loud; given to vehement outcry

9. profound

i. not straightforward or candid; giving a false appearance of frankness

10. cajole

j. showing intellectual penetration or emotional depth

11. censor

k. characterized by dignity and propriety

Vocabulary 5

verdict • complement • mystique • substantiate • exhilarating • co
erce • bereave • lethargic • derogatory • viable • blatant •
irascible

Pairing Quiz 5

1. verdict

a. the findings of a jury on issues of fact submitted to it for decision; can be used in formulating a judgment

2. coerce

b. a word or phrase used to complete a grammatical construction

3. bereave

c. an aura of heightened value or interest or meaning surrounding a person or thing

4. irascible

d. to establish or strengthen as with new evidence or facts

5. complement

e. fill with sublime emotion

6. derogatory

f. to cause to do through pressure or necessity, by physical, moral or intellectual means

7. viable

g. to deprive through death

8. blatant

h. deficient in alertness or activity

9. exhilarating

i. expressive of low opinion

10. mystique

j. capable of being done with means at hand and circumstances as they are

11. substantiate

k. without any attempt at concealment; completely obvious

12. lethargic

l. quickly aroused to anger

Vocabulary 6

buttress • effrontery • bourgeois • oscillate • beguile • admonish •
reiterate • tractable • bestial • abject • laborious • distraught

Pairing Quiz 6

1. oscillate

2. beguile

3. bestial

4. admonish

5. reiterate

6. laborious

7. abject

8. distraught

9. tractable

10. bourgeois

11. effrontery

12. buttress

a. a support usually of stone or brick; supports the wall of a building

b. audacious (even arrogant) behavior that you have no right to

c. a capitalist who engages in industrial commercial enterprise

d. be undecided about something; waver between conflicting positions or courses of action

e. influence by slyness

f. to admonish or counsel in terms of someone's behavior

g. to say, state, or perform again

h. easily managed (controlled or taught or molded)

i. resembling a beast; showing lack of human sensibility

j. of the most contemptible kind

k. characterized by effort to the point of exhaustion; especially physical effort

l. deeply agitated especially from emotion

Vocabulary 7

perfidy • thwart • gaudiness • curtail • saturate • bilk • vituperate •
enormous • latent • ostentatious • imperious • impregnable

Pairing Quiz 7

1. thwart	a. betrayal of a trust
2. vituperate	b. to prevent one from accomplishing something
3. enormous	c. tasteless showiness
4. impregnable	d. place restrictions on
5. latent	e. cause (a chemical compound, vapor, solution, magnetic material) to unite with the greatest possible amount of another substance
6. gaudiness	f. cheat somebody out of what is due, especially money
7. saturate	g. spread negative information about
8. ostentatious	h. extraordinarily large in size or extent or amount or power or degree; that a whole civilization should be dependent on technology"- Walter Lippman
9. curtail	i. potentially existing but not presently evident or realized
10. bilk	j. intended to attract notice and impress others
11. imperious	k. having or showing arrogant superiority to and disdain of those one views as unworthy
12. perfidy	l. immune to attack; incapable of being tampered with

Vocabulary 8

caulk • zeal • chauvinism • impair • flout • dote • acquaint • irrefut
able • avid • tangible • malevolent • colossal

Pairing Quiz 8

1. zeal

a. a waterproof filler and sealant that is used in building and repair to make watertight

2. dote

b. a feeling of strong eagerness (usually in favor of a person or cause)

3. caulk

c. fanatical patriotism

4. avid

d. make worse or less effective

5. acquaint

e. treat with contemptuous disregard

6. flout

f. be foolish or senile due to old age

7. tangible

g. cause to come to know personally

8. impair

h. impossible to deny or disprove

9. irrefutable

i. (often followed by `for') ardently or excessively desirous

10. malevolent

j. perceptible by the senses especially the sense of touch

11. colossal

k. wishing or appearing to wish evil to others; arising from intense ill will or hatred

12. chauvinism

l. so great in size or force or extent as to elicit awe

Vocabulary 9

repugnance • talon • reparation • compassionate •
disenfranchised • juxtaposed • emulate • anxious • resonant •
distraught • latent • parochial

Pairing Quiz 9

1. juxtaposed	a. intense aversion
2. resonant	b. a sharp hooked claw especially on a bird of prey
3. parochial	c. compensation (given or received) for an insult or injury
4. emulate	d. share the suffering of
5. talon	e. to deprive of voting rights
6. disenfranchised	f. placed side by side
7. anxious	g. to strive to equal or match, especially by imitating
8. latent	h. eagerly desirous
9. repugnance	i. continuing to sound
10. reparation	j. deeply agitated especially from emotion
11. compassionate	k. potentially existing but not presently evident or realized
12. distraught	l. relating to or supported by or located in a parish

Vocabulary 10

usury • tarnish • precursor • emaciated • abase • emulate • loll •
somber • demure • tractable • tawdry • witting

Pairing Quiz 10

1. emaciated

2. precursor

3. witting

4. demure

5. tractable

6. emulate

7. usury

8. loll

9. tawdry

10. abase

11. somber

12. tarnish

a. an exorbitant or unlawful rate of interest

b. discoloration of metal surface caused by oxidation

c. a substance from which another substance is formed (especially by a metabolic reaction)

d. cause to grow thin or weak

e. cause to feel shame; hurt the pride of

f. to strive to equal or match, especially by imitating

g. hang loosely or laxly

h. lacking brightness or color; dull

i. affectedly modest or shy especially in a playful or provocative way

j. easily managed (controlled or taught or molded)

k. tastelessly showy

l. aware or knowing

Answer Key

Pairing Quiz 1

1. e
2. c
3. j
4. d
5. a
6. i
7. g
8. k
9. b
10. f
11. l
12. h

Pairing Quiz 2

1. g
2. d
3. i
4. f
5. e
6. c
7. j
8. a
9. l
10. k
11. h
12. b

Pairing Quiz 3

1. a
2. i
3. l
4. h
5. g
6. c
7. j
8. b

9. f
10. d
11. e
12. k

Pairing Quiz 4

1. c
2. h
3. b
4. e
5. i
6. k
7. d
8. g
9. j
10. f
11. a

Pairing Quiz 5

1. a
2. f
3. g
4. l
5. b
6. i
7. j
8. k
9. e
10. c
11. d
12. h

Pairing Quiz 6

1. d
2. e
3. i
4. f

5. g
6. k
7. j
8. l
9. h
10. c
11. b
12. a

Pairing Quiz 7

1. b
2. g
3. h
4. l
5. i
6. c
7. e
8. j
9. d
10. f
11. k
12. a

Pairing Quiz 8

1. b
2. f
3. a
4. i
5. g
6. e
7. j
8. d
9. h
10. k
11. l
12. c

Pairing Quiz 9

1. f
2. i
3. l
4. g
5. b
6. e
7. h
8. k
9. a
10. c
11. d
12. j

Pairing Quiz 10

1. d
2. c
3. l
4. i
5. j
6. f
7. a
8. g
9. k
10. e
11. h
12. b

Additional Reading

Here are some examples of classic English-language novels for those who wish to further their vocabulary studies with outside reading:

- *Alice's Adventures in Wonderland* by Lewis Carroll
- *1984* by George Orwell
- *The Hobbit* by J.R.R. Tolkien
- *The Great Gatsby* by F. Scott Fitzgerald
- *Of Mice and Men* by John Steinbeck
- *Lord of the Flies* by William Golding
- *The Old Man and the Sea* by Ernest Hemingway
- *The Secret Garden* by Frances Hodgson Burnett

About the Authors

Enrica Claire Tan is a junior writer who aspires to one day become a renowned writer and computer scientist. She believes that good language and communication are some of the most important (and underappreciated) skills for admittance to the best colleges in the nation.

To help language learners improve their vocabulary, Enrica designed a learning system that involves embedding vocabulary words into short stories to make them more contextual. This method helps the language learner both build associative memory *and* improve comprehension – especially when combined with studying dictionary definitions and completing practice sets.

Michelle Ranken is a Seattle-based writer, editor and content creator. She has a bachelor's degree in political science from the University of Washington and has written on a variety of topics, including STEM (science, technology, engineering and math) and education in Washington state, to politics and restaurant reviews. She believes that the key to successful learning is to stay engaged in the material, which usually means making it fun!

Dr. Henry Tan is a computer scientist with expertise in Natural Language Processing (NLP), Data Mining, and Machine Learning. He obtained his PhD in computer science from the University of Technology in Sydney, Australia and has developed a large-scale industrial search engine and machine learning systems for Microsoft and Google.

Henry believes that when it comes to a successful career, having excellent language, communication and public-speaking skills can easily set you apart from the crowd.

Made in the USA
Middletown, DE
20 September 2023

38797460R00073